# DEATHLY (DE)VICES

"Pastor Dillon T. Thornton has done something almost unimaginable in today's hyperconnected world: he's gone off social media—cold turkey. But *Deathly (De)Vices* isn't an instruction manual on how you can do the same. Instead, it's a thoughtful exploration of how our smartphones can warp our souls. Dillon uses the seven capital vices—vainglory, envy, sloth, avarice, wrath, gluttony, and lust—to not only shine a light on the technology, but on our own hearts. A challenging, engrossing read!"

—CHRIS CASTALDO, Lead Pastor,
New Covenant Church of Naperville, Illinois

"While critics of today's technologies abound, Dillon Thornton offers a rare treat: thoughtful and clear-eyed teachings of Scripture that reveal God's nature as a way to call us to face the soul malformations that are at stake in our everyday uses of digital devices and social media. A terrific resource for preaching and discipleship, *Deathly (De)Vices* is an accessible go-to primer that persuasively refreshes such ancient terms as avarice and sloth for our digital lives today."

—FELICIA SONG, author of *Restless Devices: Recovering Personhood, Presence, and Place in the Digital Age*

"The beauty of Dillon Thornton's excellent book, *Deathly (De)Vices*, is that it calls out the seven capital sins that mark our hearts and lives and mar our discipleship of Jesus, both for those who are glued to their devices and the digitally disengaged. The book provides a discipleship health-check with warmth and humility, rich biblical insights, and practical advice. It avoids simplistic all-or-nothing approaches to technology, instead encouraging wisdom, godliness, and greater abiding in Jesus."

—CLAIRE S. SMITH, author of *The Appearing of God Our Savior: A Theology of 1 and 2 Timothy and Titus*

"Our relationship to technology is this century's most urgent question of theology and discipleship. With a scholar's insight and a pastor's care, Dillon Thornton offers crucial wisdom for navigating the complex and pernicious world of devices, media, and entertainment. By drawing our attention to the malformation we invite into our lives when we uncritically embrace technological trends, Thornton sets our sights towards higher joys and a more faithful, more human way to live."

>   —Zachary Wagner, Director of Programs,
>   Center for Pastor Theologians

# Deathly (De)Vices

Our Ever-Present Portals to Seven Ancient Sins

↡

DILLON T. THORNTON

CASCADE *Books* • Eugene, Oregon

DEATHLY (DE)VICES
Our Ever-Present Portals to Seven Ancient Sins

Copyright © 2026 Dillon T. Thornton. All rights reserved. Except for brief quotations in critical publications or reviews, no part of this book may be reproduced in any manner without prior written permission from the publisher. Write: Permissions, Wipf and Stock Publishers, 199 W. 8th Ave., Suite 3, Eugene, OR 97401.

Cascade Books
An Imprint of Wipf and Stock Publishers
199 W. 8th Ave., Suite 3
Eugene, OR 97401

www.wipfandstock.com

PAPERBACK ISBN: 979-8-3852-1271-2
HARDCOVER ISBN: 979-8-3852-1272-9
EBOOK ISBN: 979-8-3852-1273-6

*Cataloguing-in-Publication data:*

Names: Thornton, Dillon T. [author]

Title: Deathly (de)vices : our ever-present portals to seven ancient sins / by Dillon T. Thornton.

Description: Eugene, OR: Cascade Books, 2026 | Includes bibliographical references.

Identifiers: ISBN 979-8-3852-1271-2 (paperback) | ISBN 979-8-3852-1272-9 (hardcover) | ISBN 979-8-3852-1273-6 (ebook)

Subjects: LCSH: Deadly sins. | Vices. | Internet—Social aspects. | Ethics. | Information technology—Social aspects. | Mass media—Technological innovations—Social aspects. | Spiritual formation. | Christian life.

Classification: BV4511 T467 2026 (print) | BV4511 (ebook)

All Scripture quotations are from the *ESV® Bible (The Holy Bible, English Standard Version®)*, Copyright © 2001 by Crossway, a publishing ministry of Good News Publishers. Used by permission. All rights reserved.

Wendell Berry, "The Peace of Wild Things" from New Collected Poems. Copyright © 2012 by Wendell Berry. Reprinted with the permission of The Permissions Company, LLC on behalf of Counterpoint Press, counterpointpress.com.

To the families of Faith Community Church.
To change the world, begin with your own platoon.

The cost of a thing is the amount of . . . life which is required to be exchanged for it, immediately or in the long run.

—Henry David Thoreau, *Walden*

# Contents

**Acknowledgments** xi

1. Introduction: "Abide in Me, and I in You" 1
   *Including the question: Is technology good, bad, or neutral?*

2. Vainglory: Whose Glory Story Is This? 11
   *Including a brief history of screens*

3. Envy: Seeing Everyone, Everywhere, All the Time 26
   *Including the rise of selfie-based social media*

4. Sloth: Being Lazy at Love 40
   *Including how our technologies hook us*

5. Avarice: All Is Advertisement 57
   *Including the inception of the influencer industry*

6. Wrath: Tension Gets Attention 71
   *Including how algorithms elicit anger*

7. Gluttony: Taking Control of Our Information Intake 86
   *Including how to develop discernment online*

8. Lust: From *I Love Lucy* to Full Frontal Nudity 103
   *Including how to fight the porn hydra*

9. Conclusion: "Now I See" 117

**Bibliography** 121

# Acknowledgments

I'M GRATEFUL TO THE families of Faith Community Church for providing the pastoral context in which my understanding of technology and spiritual formation could develop.

To the elders of Faith Church—Darrin Anderson, Todd Runkle, Dan Savarese, and Brian Wyant—who provided me with a generous sabbatical, during which I wrote a sizable portion of this book.

To the editorial team at Wipf and Stock, whose sagacious suggestions made my writing clearer.

To my careful readers—Brad Greer, Kyle Cullum, Michelle Cullum, and Felicia Wu Song. Each improved this book by providing comments on sections of the penultimate draft.

To my sons—Aidan Thomas and Cullen Timothy—who reluctantly supply the arsenal of illustrations I use in my preaching, teaching, and writing.

Most of all, I'm grateful to Jamie, my co-creator, co-adventurer, my Beauty, my Lúthien.

# 1

# Introduction

"Abide in Me, and I in You"

## THE MAD SCIENTIST

I ONCE WORKED WITH a man who referred to me as "the mad scientist." I'm no scientist, and as far I can tell, I'm not mad. But he insisted on this nickname because, in his words, "You always have an idea." By divine design, I'm a thinker and tinkerer, an inquirer and investigator, a wonderer and researcher. At the beginning of 2023, one of those nagging ideas came to me, a mental mosquito that just wouldn't leave me alone. It was a series of questions, really: "What would I notice about myself if I took an extended absence from social media? Would I become a better human being? Would I be more present with those who are most important to me? Would I feel disconnected from the world? Would I lose my influence as a pastor? Would I ever have another opportunity to publish a book?"[1] I decided to find out.

---

1. Beaty, *Celebrities for Jesus*, 102–3, writes, "The pressure to turn a profit gives platform an outsize role in who gets book deals. Quality of writing, educational credentials, and hard-won wisdom are not enough to get a contract. Writers are told they *must* also have platforms. Some author hopefuls find that creating a platform is like a second job. By contrast, someone with a large social media following, who can't write or doesn't have much to say, will find plenty of publishers and agents who want to publish their book. Numbers rule" (emphasis original).

What started as an experiment spanning a few weeks stretched into a few months and eventually to an entire year. At the time of the publication of this book, it will be over two years since I have set digital foot on Facebook, Instagram, Twitter (I missed the rebranding to X), or TikTok. Throughout the experiment, here are a few things I've noticed about myself, in no particular order:

- I'm *more* present with my family.
- I'm *more* reflective and productive. (Who knew a person could be both?)
- I spend *less* time thinking about myself: less pride, less concern for the bits of my existence that the whole world simply must know about. Post this, share that.
- I spend *less* time thinking about others in a negative way: less envy, less anger, less unforgiveness, less lust.
- I spend *less* time shopping online; I'm *more* content.
- I spend *more* time on problems I can help solve, rather than fixating on issues that are far away.
- I spend *more* time getting to know people—real people—rather than drawing conclusions based on their social media posts.

In this season of disengagement, I think I've become a better human being, a more faithful follower of Christ—though still imperfect. I haven't been condemned to rank ignorance; I've simply found other and better ways of getting information. Regarding my influence as a pastor, I'm happy to report that through the preaching of God's word and activity of the Holy Spirit, our church has continued to grow. People in our city continue to repent of their sins and look with faith to Jesus Christ. And as for my future as a writer, well, here I am, dear reader: ink still inching along.

Maybe social media isn't all it's cracked up to be.

Introduction

# "ABIDE IN ME, AND I IN YOU" —JESUS (AND YOUR IPHONE)

While working on this project, I did some part-time teaching at a local Christian school. The teaching gig allowed me to minister to students during some of their most formative years, and it compelled me to become a better "translator." C. S. Lewis contends that the power to translate a complex subject into everyday speech—or we might say "middle school speech"—is the test of having really understood the subject at hand.[2] The portion of the curriculum I developed for the school covers the storyline of Scripture, basics of spiritual formation, an introduction to apologetics, and systematic theology. In the spiritual formation class, I included a section on technology, which middle and high school students usually have a keen desire to discuss, some thinking themselves experts on the topic since they've spent more time with their iPhones than with every flesh-and-blood person in their lives combined. I began our discussion of technology with a question: "Is technology good, bad, or neutral?" Nearly every student responded, "Neutral." But, truth be told, it's a trick question.

In his oft-quoted first law of technology, Melvin Kranzberg states, "Technology is neither good nor bad; nor is it neutral."[3] By this Kranzberg means, to use Tony Reinke's gloss, "We can't drop a gadget into an ethics machine and wait for it to come out the other side, stamped as 'virtuous' or 'sinful' . . . . In reality, the inherent sinfulness or virtue of a given technology is often vague until an actor wields the tool with intent."[4] The same technology can have different results when introduced in different contexts or in different ways. Nuclear technology, for example, offers the prospect of unlimited energy resources, but also the possibility of worldwide

---

2. Lewis, "Christian Apologetics," 155.

3. Kranzberg, "Technology and History," 545. Similarly, Postman, *Amusing Ourselves to Death*, 84, writes, "Only those who know nothing of the history of technology believe that a technology is entirely neutral."

4. Reinke, *God, Technology, and the Christian Life*, 69–70.

## Deathly (De)Vices

destruction.[5] To help us catch his drift, Kranzberg tells a short story. Once, after a concert, a lady rushed to the great violinist Fritz Kreisler and said, "Maestro, your violin makes such beautiful music!" Kreisler held his violin up to his ear and replied, "I don't hear any music coming out of it."[6] *When man wields technology, and especially as he wields it over time, we see more clearly the good or the bad.* The duty of the historian, Kranzberg says, is "to compare short-term versus long-term results, the utopian hopes versus the spotted actuality, the what-might-have-been against what actually happened."[7]

We now have decades of usage to consider, twenty to thirty years of men and women, boys and girls, wielding personal devices that allow essentially uninterrupted access to email, social media, videos, games, and infinitely more.[8] What's your anecdotal assessment of our situation? In your judgment, does the generation raised on devices seem to be more human, more humane? Do *any of us* who live online seem to be more alert to spiritual realities, more focused on the kingdom of God?

Ardent tech-optimists argue that our devices are not the problem. "Technology doesn't *determine* human behavior," they will say. "Devices merely open a door. They do not compel one to enter." However, it's important for us to see how technology makes certain worlds and behaviors more imaginable and desirable than others.[9] As Kranzberg points out, "An open door is *an invitation*." "Besides," he explains, "who decides which doors to open—and, once one has entered the door, are not one's future directions guided by the contours of the corridor or chamber into

---

5. Kranzberg, "Technology and History," 547.
6. Kranzberg, "Technology and History," 558.
7. Kranzberg, "Technology and History," 547–48.
8. Throughout this work, I'll use a host of words—*device, internet, social internet, social media, digital technology*, etc.—to refer to one main reality, which James, *Digital Liturgies*, 12, helpfully defines as "*the disembodied electronic environment that we enter through connected devices for the purpose of accessing information, relationships, and media that are not available to us in a physical format*" (emphasis original).
9. Song, *Restless Devices*, 26.

INTRODUCTION

which one has stepped? Equally important, once one has crossed the threshold, can one turn back?"[10] By God's grace, I believe we can. But it will require a collective coming to our senses. *We need eyes to see what untempered attachment to our devices is doing to us.* "Not everything that is faced can be changed," James Baldwin once said, "but nothing can be changed until it is faced."[11] This is where I hope the present work will be of some help.[12]

We must begin to think of our devices in terms of *spiritual formation*. Seven times in John's Gospel Jesus says, "I am," and then fills in the blank with a metaphor that reveals something important about who he is and what he came to accomplish for us. The seventh of these sayings occurs in John 15:4–5:

> Abide in me, and I in you. As the branch cannot bear fruit by itself, unless it abides in the vine, neither can you, unless you abide in me. I am the vine; you are the branches. Whoever abides in me and I in him, he it is that bears much fruit, for apart from me you can do nothing.

This is Spiritual Formation 101. Jesus says to his followers, "Apart from me you can do nothing." Not, "Apart from me you can do a few things." Not, "Apart from me you'll accomplish only lesser goals." But, "Apart from me you can do *nothing*."

Our devices assert themselves similarly. "Apart from me," my iPhone claims, "you can do nothing. You can't make friends. You can't find a spouse. You can't be productive enough to get promoted. You can't remain knowledgeable about the world." And on and on it avers.

At the beginning of v. 4, Jesus says, "Abide in me, and I in you." The term "abide" is used ten times in this passage. It's the key word of the text. Abiding in Jesus is more than simply believing in him, though certainly it includes this. Abiding is living in union with Jesus, sharing his power, thoughts, emotions, and intentions.

---

10. Kranzberg, "Technology and History," 545 (emphasis added).
11. Cited in Hari, *Stolen Focus*, 14–15.
12. Other works that deal with the harmful spiritual effects of our devices include Reinke, *12 Ways Your Phone Is Changing You*; Song, *Restless Devices*; James, *Digital Liturgies*; Martin, *Wolf in Their Pockets*.

# Deathly (De)Vices

This sharing involves *choosing*: we must decide to do things that expose us to Jesus' heart and ways, things like prayer and personal Bible reading, regular fellowship with a small group of believers and the weekly gathering of a local church. These practices, and others like them, are sometimes called spiritual disciplines, but we might also refer to them as rhythms of abiding. When we abide in Christ, we flourish, producing plentiful and beautiful fruit. "Whoever abides in me and I in him, he it is that bears much fruit" (v. 5). This is Jesus' promise to us.

Our devices mimic Jesus' call to discipleship: "Abide in me, and I in you."[13] Abiding in this sense means living in the unending digital flow. This, too, involves *choosing*: we must decide to do things that keep us in a state of permanent connectivity. The disciple of the lord called Digital has his own set of spiritual disciplines or rhythms of abiding. And these practices, too, lead to formation—albeit *de*-formation. The disciple of this ilk will find that he is incrementally yet definitively fashioned into a new creation.[14] But not every new creation is a pretty one. Read *Frankenstein*. When we abide in our devices—clinging to them in desperation, never allowing ourselves to be cut off from their power—an evil abundance will appear. "Whoever abides in me and I in him, he it is that bears much fruit." This is your iPhone's promise.

## THAT EVIL ABUNDANCE: THE SEVEN CAPITAL VICES

My primary aim in this work is to illuminate some of the ways our devices incite the so-called seven deadly sins, more accurately called the seven capital vices: vainglory, envy, sloth, avarice, wrath, gluttony, and lust.[15] A vice or its counterpart, a virtue, is a habit-

---

13. I'm grateful to Song, "Digital Life and Social Media as Secular Liturgy," 207, for helping me make this powerful connection.

14. Song, *Restless Devices*, 2.

15. To manage expectations, this book is not intended to be a biblical-theological treatment of technology in general, but a more focused attempt to demonstrate how certain technologies tend to stir vice within our hearts. For

# INTRODUCTION

ual disposition or character trait, a *way of being*. We can cultivate positive or negative character traits over time through repeated actions. Virtues are "excellences" of character; vices are failures of character. The former are ways of living well in God's world; the latter are ways of living poorly, having a corruptive and destructive effect on ourselves and others.[16]

As far as historians can tell, a list of vices similar to the one I use in this book was first compiled by the fourth-century writer Evagrius of Pontus. Evagrius joined a monastic community, deliberately withdrawing from the wiles of the world. It's a bit ironic that, there in the desert, a member of this community created with the hope of a deeper experience of God, Evagrius and his fellow monks became better acquainted with their own sin.[17] By the thirteenth century, Thomas Aquinas develops the list I follow here.[18] In her insightful book *Glittering Vices*, Rebecca Konyndyk DeYoung clarifies the label "capital vices." The Christian tradition singled out these vices, she says, "because they are the '*source vices*,' vices that serve as an ever-bubbling wellspring of many others."[19] If we picture a spiritual battle, these vices are the generals, with other vices serving as their foot soldiers. Or, to use an image common in the Middle Ages, if we picture a forbidding tree, these vices are the main branches. From each of the seven grows many smaller branches, and each of these likewise bears toxic fruit.[20]

In the chapters that follow, we'll look more closely at this tree, and, relying on the Spirit to bring out our inner lumberjack, take an axe to the branches. Each chapter will travel roughly the same path. First, we'll conduct an anatomy of one of the vices. What

---

those interested in a more comprehensive treatment of technology, I recommend Reinke, *God, Technology, and the Christian Life*.

16. DeYoung, *Glittering Vices*, 7–8.

17. Willimon, *Sinning Like a Christian*, 3.

18. For a discussion of the development of the vice lists, including Evagrius, Cassian, Gregory I, and Aquinas's contributions, see DeYoung, *Glittering Vices*, 21–39.

19. DeYoung, *Glittering Vices*, 30 (emphasis added).

20. DeYoung, *Glittering Vices*, 31.

## Deathly (De)Vices

does Scripture teach us about it? What does it look like? The capital vices are less like a broken arm, easily spotted and rather simple to treat, and more like a cancer, hidden within and much more challenging to eradicate. Naming the disease, seeing and understanding the vice, is the necessary first step.

Second, we'll consider how our devices incite the vice. Sin has infected humanity since the time of Gen 3, and lists of capital vices have circulated since the fourth century. But the innovations of our day constitute a unique challenge. In our technological moment, most of us have on our persons—nearly every second of the day—a device that possesses great power, including the power to awaken the vices. *In my pocket I have a portal that can carry me to countless evil places.*[21] Evagrius had sinful tendencies in his heart. We have sinful tendencies in our hearts, and an almost omnipresent technology with the capacity to incite those tendencies. We're like recovering alcoholics who live in a bar. Not for one moment can we let down our guards.

Third and finally, we'll seek to develop our theological understanding and spiritual practices, rhythms of abiding in Jesus, which will counter the vice's power. The only lasting solution to being carried away by the vice-inducing digital flow is to become anchored in and enlivened by the scriptural story.

## WHEN IN PARIS

I wrote a sizeable portion of this book while on sabbatical in the summer of 2024. During this season of research and respite, my family spent some time in Paris. My oldest son has an affinity for the Eiffel Tower, so I arranged a guided tour for the family. Our tour guide was excellent and the tower itself unforgettable. We climbed to the top of the 300-meter structure, weighing over 10,000 tons, with its 1,665 steps. We learned about the construction of the

---

21. Smith, *Internet Is Not What You Think It Is*, 18, writes, "Whatever your habits and your duties, your public responsibilities and secret desires, they are all concentrated as never before into a single device, a filter, and a portal for the conduct of nearly every kind of human life today."

## Introduction

tower from 1887 to 1889, how many colors it's been over the years, how long it takes to paint the tower, and how much it costs to paint such a colossal construction (3 million euros!). The meeting place for our tour was an alley a few blocks away from the tower. The alley dead ends at a thicket, which provides a splendid lower border for the tower. Off the beaten path, no traffic, it's the perfect place to sit quietly and appreciate this unparalleled feat of engineering. Apparently, it's also the perfect place to make a TikTok video. At some point, the Instagrammers and TikTokers found this magical spot, and now they clamor for control of it. While we waited for our tour, I observed three teenage girls do dozens and dozens of takes, trying to get their dance moves just right. I watched two women dressed to the nines take picture after picture in front of the tower. It seems they had gotten all dressed up, not for a fancy dinner or show, but to stand in this alley—for hours—stockpiling selfies for their social media accounts. I couldn't help but wonder what Gustave Eiffel would think about all of this. What would he say about his feat of engineering becoming "fodder that will merely draw attention to our feed?"[22]

We had a similar experience when we visited the Louvre Museum. The Louvre is massive. You could spend days there and still see only half the art. One long hallway leads to another, and then to another, every wall covered with paintings. Some sections of the museum are more popular than others. I felt bad for those hallways with hardly any people in them. These paintings were like those players on an NBA bench who never get playing time: special enough to be *close* to the action. Then there were the sections of the Louvre that were swarming with people. By far the most crowded room was the one containing Leonardo da Vinci's *Mona Lisa*. If you've never seen the *Mona Lisa* in person, spoiler alert: she's tiny. It's one of the smaller paintings in the Louvre. But it was surrounded by an ocean of people, with no queue or any civil way of getting an up-close look. I watched from the back of the room as person after person fought his or her way through the ocean, doing whatever it took to lock eyes with Da Vinci's masterpiece.

22. Song, *Restless Devices*, 78.

## Deathly (De)Vices

I watched as they all did the exact same thing: they fought to the front, looked at the painting for half a second, and then turned their backs on it, raised their iPhones, snapped a selfie, and fought their way out.[23] Again, just fodder to draw attention to the feed.

I left Paris with a profound appreciation for the art of the city and with another of those pesky questions buzzing in my mind: "How did we become so vain?"

---

23. Hari, *Stolen Focus*, 8–9, reports having the same experience.

## 2

# Vainglory

## Whose Glory Story Is This?

### THE TOOLS THAT MAKE US

THE IPHONE WAS INTRODUCED to the world in January 2007. By January 2021, over 1.65 billion units had been sold, making it the most successful product of any kind ever made.[1] We often fail to notice the thing that's right in front of us. A fish doesn't see the water; he just swims. If you were born after 2007, then you've never known a world without an iPhone. If you're a late Millennial or Gen Z-er, then your adult life has been lived on devices. Many of us don't see the digital waters in which we're immersed; we just swim. And that's the problem.

I'm not one of those laughable people who thinks we need to destroy everything but typewriters before AI takes over the world. If the robots rise up, I'm pretty sure the rednecks can take them. I'm not against technology as a category.[2] I'm writing this chapter

---

1. Smith, *(Un)Intentional*, 4. Dyer, *People of the Screen*, 80, reports that among US adults, smartphone ownership has risen from 33 percent in 2011 to 77 percent in 2016, and to 81 percent in 2019.

2. Reinke, *God, Technology, and the Christian Life*, 14, explains, "Technology is applied science and amplified power. It's art, method, know-how, formulas, and expertise. The word *technology* is built on the root *techne-* or *technique*. We amplify our native powers through new techniques" (italics original).

## Deathly (De)Vices

on my MacBook Pro, AirPods in, while sitting in my climate-controlled home, sipping a pour-over coffee made with a gooseneck kettle that has a to-the-degree temperature control—and I wouldn't write, *couldn't* write, any other way. I'm thankful for many of the tools we wield. Yet, I'm concerned about what certain technologies like the social internet do to us when we swim in them mindlessly. Here's the thing about technology: it never travels alone. Always, it brings consequences. Some good; some bad. Some intentional; some unintentional. But always consequences.

Wendell Berry has an essay titled "Horse-Drawn Tools and the Doctrine of Labor Saving." Sounds like a riveting read, I know, but it's actually very insightful. Berry uses the example of the tractor to help us see the unintended consequences of technological development. "The coming of the tractor made it possible for a farmer to do more work, but not better. And there comes a point, as we know, when *more* begins to imply *worse*."[3] He continues:

> The increase of power has made it possible for one worker to crop an enormous acreage, but for this "efficiency" the country has paid a high price. From 1946 to 1976, because fewer people were needed, the farm population declined from thirty million to nine million; the rapid movement of these millions into the cities greatly aggravated that complex of problems which we now call the "urban crisis," and the land is suffering for want of the care of those absent families. The coming of a tool, then, can be a cultural event of great influence and power. Once that is understood, it is no longer possible to be simple-minded about technological progress. It is no longer possible to ask, What is a good tool? without

---

3. Berry, "Horse-Drawn Tools and the Doctrine of Labor Saving," 474 (emphasis original). I think of Dyer's recent research, which reveals that while reading on a screen has a positive effect on reading frequency, it has a negative effect on comprehension. Screen-based Bible students read more often and have better completion rates for reading plans, but they understand less. To use Berry's terms, *more* reading has led to *worse* reading. See Dyer, *People of the Screen*, 160–80.

asking at the same time, How *well* does it work? and, What is its influence?⁴

Elsewhere, Berry points to the profound influence and irony of the interstate: "The interstate cut through farms. It divided neighbor from neighbor. It made distant what had been close, and close what had been distant."⁵ Saying hello to the ability to travel widely, from one side of the country to the other, meant saying goodbye to the ability to walk easily from one farm to another. States united; neighbors divided. Technology giveth, and technology taketh away. Every innovation carries its own negativity. If you dig a pit, you can fall into it. If you quarry stones, they can roll down and crush you. When you invent the ship, you also invent the shipwreck. When you invent electricity, you also invent electrocution.⁶

Berry's questions, "What is a good tool? How well does it work? And what is its influence?" are important ones for every age, for every technological development.⁷ I'm especially concerned with the final question. How are our digital tools changing our world? Changing us? We're inclined to think that *we shape technology*, which, of course, is true. But it's also true that *technology shapes us.*⁸ A common conception is that technology is a neutral tool. If the social internet user consumes wholesome content, then the web is friend, not foe, right? In his book *Digital Liturgies*, Samuel James argues otherwise. "Rather than being a neutral tool," James writes, "the internet (particularly the social internet) is an epistemological environment—a spiritual and intellectual habitat—that creates in its members particular ways of thinking,

---

4. Berry, "Horse-Drawn Tools and the Doctrine of Labor Saving," 474 (emphasis original). Since the COVID pandemic, the flight has been *away from cities*. See Goldberg, "ZIP Code Shift." Time will tell what this rapid movement will aggravate.

5. Berry, *Jayber Crow*, 281.

6. Reinke, *God, Technology, and the Christian Life*, 134.

7. See also Berry, "Why I Am Not Going to Buy a Computer," 726–27. Here, he gives his standards for technological innovation, the final of which is "it should not replace or disrupt anything good that already exists, and this includes family and community relationships."

8. James, *Digital Liturgies*, 24.

feeling, and believing."[9] He goes on to suggest, "Rather than thinking of the web and social media as merely neutral tools that merely do whatever users ask of them, it is better to think of them as kinds of spaces that are continually shaping us to think, feel, communicate, and live in certain ways."[10] Our digital tools make us. Our devices disciple us. As James puts it, "The web preaches to our brains and to our hearts. So the question naturally becomes, 'What is the web preaching?'"[11] My contention is that one of its primary appeals is "Come, let us make a name for ourselves."

## TWO VAINGLORY STORIES

The first capital vice, vainglory, is not a common word in our vocabularies. We might be inclined to equate vainglory with pride, but they're slightly different. Pride is concerned with excellence. Vainglory is concerned with appearance. The prideful person wants superior status. He or she values being number one on the team or in a certain field of study, for example. The vainglorious person wants superior notice—with or without the excellence. In the movie *Glass Onion*, the antagonist Miles Bron, played by Edward Norton, says repeatedly, "I want to be responsible for something that gets talked about in the same breath as the Mona Lisa. Forever."[12] His lack of specificity is telling: "I want to be responsible for *something* that gets talked about...." The nature of the achievement matters little; it's attention that drives him. The vainglorious person seeks whatever will bring him the most applause. Her obsession is recognition. Image is everything.[13]

---

    9. James, *Digital Liturgies*, 9. Similarly, Martin, *Wolf in Their Pockets*, 11–22. To Christian leaders, Martin says, "Social media likely shapes the people you love and disciple more than you do" (11).

    10. James, *Digital Liturgies*, 10.

    11. James, *Digital Liturgies*, 66 (emphasis original).

    12. Johnson, *Glass Onion*.

    13. DeYoung, *Glittering Vices*, 44–47.

The builders of Babel wanted to be responsible for something that was talked about both far and wide, on earth and in heaven. The infamous story is recorded in Gen 11:1–9:

> Now the whole earth had one language and the same words. And as people migrated from the east, they found a plain in the land of Shinar and settled there. And they said to one another, "Come, let us make bricks, and burn them thoroughly." And they had brick for stone, and bitumen for mortar. Then they said, "Come, let us build ourselves a city and a tower with its top in the heavens, and let us make a name for ourselves, lest we be dispersed over the face of the whole earth." And the LORD came down to see the city and the tower, which the children of man had built. And the LORD said, "Behold, they are one people, and they have all one language, and this is only the beginning of what they will do. And nothing that they propose to do will now be impossible for them. Come, let us go down and there confuse their language, so that they may not understand one another's speech." So the LORD dispersed them from there over the face of all the earth, and they left off building the city. Therefore its name was called Babel, because there the LORD confused the language of all the earth. And from there the LORD dispersed them over the face of all the earth.

It begins with the human work of construction. United by a common language and utilizing the technology of their day, the people say, "Come, let us build ourselves a city and a tower with its top in the heavens, and let us make a name for ourselves, lest we be dispersed over the face of the whole earth" (v. 4).[14] They describe their project to one another as if it will be the ultimate achievement. In the Hebrew text, the project itself is referred to as a *migdāl*, which comes from the root *gdl*, meaning "to be great." Here, *migdāl* designates the Mesopotamian ziggurat, a massive

---

14. Reinke, *God, Technology, and the Christian Life*, 39, argues that the divinely commissioned ark helped to inspire the technological advances that would lead to Babel. The same tar that was used to waterproof the ark is now employed to make the tower watertight, with its builders looking into the heavens, raising their fists, and shouting, "Good luck washing us away now!"

## Deathly (De)Vices

staircase structure.[15] The purpose of this project is clear: "Let us make a name for ourselves" (v. 4). "Name" signifies reputation or renown. The builders think the completion of such a prodigious task will secure their fame and immortality.[16] As Christopher Watkin puts it, "Their reputation will be mediated through their technology: people will know who they are when they see what they have built."[17] The builders are proud creators, self-makers—so they think.

To its builders, "Babel" meant "gate/residence of the gods."[18] They envisioned their invention lifting them into heaven. Ironically, the LORD must stoop and squint in order to see it (v. 5). This is divine sarcasm, trinitarian taunting. "The motif of descent is intended to parody the heaven-storming aspirations of humanity. The tower that they think will provide a divine elevator or a beachhead to ransack the very throne room of God is so small that God, rather than feeling threatened by it or needing it for his descent, stoops down so that he can get a better look at its thimble-like grandeur."[19] The story that began with the human work of construction concludes with the divine work of deconstruction, though not in the way we might expect. Why confuse the people's language? Why not topple the tower? Because towers can be rebuilt and built even higher. Even if the people didn't build another tower, they could have chosen some other vainglorious project. The solution must go deeper.[20] The absence of a common language means the lack of cooperation, which terminates the project. No mass communication, no mass megalomania.

Striking similarities occur in another Old Testament story, one to which Babel is not often compared: the parting of the Red Sea (Exod 14:1–31). From beginning to end, the crushing defeat of Pharaoh and his army is an event planned by God and intended

15. Waltke, *Genesis*, 179.
16. Hamilton, *Book of Genesis*, 353.
17. Watkin, *Biblical Critical Theory*, 213.
18. Waltke, *Genesis*, 178.
19. Watkin, *Biblical Critical Theory*, 209.
20. Hamilton, *Book of Genesis*, 355.

to be a testimony to his unparalleled power, bringing glory to him alone. After God's tenth strike upon Egypt, Pharaoh releases the people of Israel.[21] As the people leave, Pharaoh is left with a weakened kingdom and an intense grief. His grief turns to anger, his anger to madness. He gathers a massive army, equipped with the best weapons from Egypt's arsenal, and they pursue God's people. The period in which the exodus occurred was Egypt's golden age of imperial and military glory.[22] Pharaoh himself was the supreme commander of the armed forces, and to show himself a fearless leader often he would personally lead his army into battle, as he does in Exod 14. The Egyptian army was a rapid strike force that relied on chariots and archers. The war chariot was drawn by two horses and carried two men, a driver and a shield-bearer. The shield-bearer protected the unit; the driver navigated and then fired arrows or used a javelin at closer distances. We must understand the two sides that are about to meet on this battlefield. On the one side is Pharaoh's titanic army of professional soldiers wielding cutting-edge technology in the form of weaponry. On the other side is a population of untrained peasants, including women and children. Under normal circumstances, the people of Israel would have been no match for such a force.

To make matters worse, Israel is hemmed in by the sea. From the moment of their deliverance from slavery, God has been directing their steps (Exod 13:17–22). But why lead them here? It's a tactical disadvantage. In Exod 14:4, the LORD tells Moses why: "And I will harden Pharaoh's heart, and he will pursue [the people], and I will get glory over Pharaoh and all his host, and the Egyptians shall know that I am the LORD." Interestingly, this is the first time the word "glory" is used in Exodus, and from this point on it occurs regularly in the narrative. It is here that Pharaoh, who thinks himself glorious, will fall from on high and sink into

---

21. While commonly referred to as "the ten plagues," this is a misnomer. Most of the tragedies that befall Egypt are not diseases. The concept of "strikes"—as in the strike of a fist—better reflects the Hebrew terminology used throughout the passage.

22. See the excurses in Garrett, *Commentary on Exodus*, 388–93.

## Deathly (De)Vices

the depths of the sea. It is here that the LORD will demonstrate conclusively that he is all-powerful, all-glorious. The people must face the sea and go forward. Moses must lift his staff and extend his hand toward the water. Other than this, God's people will *do* nothing. They will *say* nothing: "you have only to be silent," Moses declares (v. 14). They will merely *see*. They're not warriors. They're not advisors. They're observers, beholders of the glory of the LORD. He will fight for them.

The LORD sends a strong wind to drive back the waters, dividing the sea, creating both the way of escape for his people and the method of dethroning Pharaoh and destroying the evil of Egypt. The sea becomes like Jell-O. "The deeps congealed" (Exod 15:8). With a wall of water to the left and a wall of water to the right, God's people march to safety. The Egyptians pursue them into the midst of the sea, but war chariots are not made for this sort of terrain. To add to their struggle, the LORD "looked down on the Egyptian forces and threw [them] into panic" (v. 24). Remember the divine sarcasm from Babel? In Gen 11:5, "the LORD came down to see the city and the tower, which the children of man had built." In Exod 14:24, the LORD stoops and squints again, this time to see puny Pharaoh and his army. In the Genesis account, God confused a vainglorious construction project. In Exodus, he confuses a vainglorious military attack. Pharaoh's army of professional soldiers wielding cutting-edge weaponry becomes a quivering mass—chariots stuck, weapons useless. Once the Israelites have passed safely through the gelatinized sea, the LORD causes the waters to return to their original state: the walls collapse into waves, and in the blink of an eye the titanic army sinks into oblivion.

Both the builders of Babel and the king of Egypt craved recognition: "Come, let us make a name for ourselves," they said. "We're writing our own glory stories" (my paraphrase). In narrative terms, rather than playing a role in God's story, they wanted God to play a supporting role in their stories.[23] They wanted to be center stage, in the spotlight. This vainglorious temptation, this

---

23. Watkin, *Biblical Critical Theory*, 208.

Babelian urge, is alive and well, though today it would be insufficient to *build* Babel. Babel must be built, photographed, posted, and liked *ad infinitum*. Indeed, if Babel hasn't been liked, followed, subscribed to, has it even been built?

## CHASING CELEBRITY

In our cultural moment, the obsession is with *celebrity*, which has been helpfully distinguished from *fame*. In Susan Douglas and Andrea McDonnell's important work on celebrity culture, they note several differences between these concepts.[24] In ancient and medieval times, fame was reserved for people with hereditary positions—a king, queen, or emperor—or for those responsible for extraordinary achievements—a successful leader or inventor, for example. "Fame was less likely to be sought than imposed as a consequence of accomplishment or office. In effect, it was a mantle one wore, not something one chased."[25] Additionally, the famous had an aura of mystery about them, a remoteness, rather than a constant visibility. No day-in-the-life-of videos revealed the eating habits of Constantine or Charlemagne or the bedtime routines of Gutenberg or Edison.[26] Men such as these became known beyond their families and friends as a result of bloodline or by means of a life well lived, not a brand well cultivated.[27] In Shakespeare's familiar lines, men are born great, achieve greatness, or have greatness thrust upon them. "It never occurred to him to mention those who hired public relations experts and press secretaries to make themselves look great."[28]

Douglas and McDonnell argue that the rise of media and communications technologies beginning in the nineteenth

---

24. Douglas and McDonnell, *Celebrity*, 1–8.

25. Douglas and McDonnell, *Celebrity*, 3, citing the historian Neal Gabler.

26. Braudy, *Frenzy of Renown*, 14, notes that in our day of incessant information, we know more about the people of the past than they usually knew about each other.

27. Beaty, *Celebrities for Jesus*, 8.

28. Boorstin, *Image*, 45.

## Deathly (De)Vices

century, especially those involving the mechanical reproduction of images, changed all of this.[29] Fame took a back seat to its "shinier, slightly obnoxious cousin," *celebrity*.[30] The word *celebrity* derives from the Latin root *celebrem*, which suggests that one is not merely celebrated, but chased by a crowd. Unlike fame, celebrity is about widespread visibility. The celebrity needn't be a big person, only a big name. In the prophetic words of Daniel Boorstin, first published in 1961, "The celebrity in the distinctive modern sense could not have existed in any earlier age, or in America before the Graphic Revolution. *The celebrity is a person who is known for his well-knownness.* His qualities—or rather his lack of qualities—illustrate our peculiar problems."[31] Anybody can become a celebrity, Boorstin says, "if only he can get into the news and stay there."[32]

Much of our daily experience tells us that we should become a celebrity if we possibly can, because it is the best—maybe the *only*—way to be.[33] As Boorstin suggests, celebrity is about media management: get in the news and stay there; build and keep an audience. It's been estimated that in the medieval world the average person saw about one hundred other people in the course of a lifetime.[34] My, how the times have changed. In the last hundred years or so we've witnessed the most decisive and rapid change with respect to one's life audience, leading us to this strange moment of history where the whole world is a stage, and everyone (it seems) is a wannabe star, chasing celebrity status. Here's how it happened....

---

29. Douglas and McDonnell, *Celebrity*, 3–4. See also Beaty, *Celebrities for Jesus*, 7–19.

30. Beaty, *Celebrities for Jesus*, 11.

31. Boorstin, *Image*, 57 (emphasis original). Burton, *Self-Made*, 216, points to the example of the Kardashians, who "became a cultural juggernaut, beloved not so much for any discernible abilities but because they seemingly lacked them."

32. Boorstin, *Image*, 60. Hund, *Influencer Industry*, 21, writes, "Celebrities are, fundamentally, a particular type of influential person whose social power is wholly dependent upon media industries."

33. Braudy, *Frenzy of Renown*, 6.

34. Braudy, *Frenzy of Renown*, 27.

By the early 1920s, there was a new and commanding type of celebrity: the movie star. Taking the movie theater for granted as we do today, it's hard to appreciate what a completely revolutionary sensory experience this was. "The cinematic apparatus—sitting in a darkened theater while watching illuminated bodies and faces larger than your own performing for you and engaging with you—enabled an entirely new and deeply compelling production of celebrity."[35] In the late 1920s, sound arrived. The sound of actors' voices added an additional layer of intimacy, making films and their stars seem all the more real. The 1930s and '40s saw the arrival of Technicolor. Walt Disney was one of the earliest adopters of this technology, producing *Flowers and Trees* in 1932. In subsequent years, Technicolor wowed audiences in films like *The Wizard of Oz* and the first feature-length animated film, *Snow White and the Seven Dwarfs*, a story to which I'll return in the next chapter. It's no surprise that the 1930s and '40s marked the height of the Hollywood era because it was during this time that audiences came to experience the stars like never before.[36] Douglas and McDonnell report that moviegoing reached its peak during the Second World War, with more than 60 percent of Americans in weekly attendance.[37]

Television brought celebrities into our homes. Unlike in theaters, where the stars appeared larger than life, television shrunk them down and beamed them into our world.[38] Given this unprecedented visual proximity, the glamour and mystique of the movie star didn't match the medium. Television stars had to be more like regular people: funnier and more attractive, perhaps, but also approachable, relatable. From the late 1940s through the '60s, television enjoyed its golden age. In 1955, 90 percent of American households had a television. It had become a fixture of domestic life.[39]

35. Douglas and McDonnell, *Celebrity*, 92.
36. Douglas and McDonnell, *Celebrity*, 110–11.
37. Douglas and McDonnell, *Celebrity*, 115.
38. Douglas and McDonnell, *Celebrity*, 162.
39. Douglas and McDonnell, *Celebrity*, 162.

## Deathly (De)Vices

The television brought the stage into the home for the first time, making entertainment "so accessible and ubiquitous that it created a desire to be entertained *all the time by everything*."[40] By the late 1990s, the internet began to enter the American home, but as long as it was bound to another bulky box—the home computer—it would be slow to surpass the power of television. It wasn't until January 9, 2007, that we caught a glimpse of what would supplant television and radically change the way we think about celebrity. When Steve Jobs introduced the iPhone, he demonstrated how customers could use the device to watch shows like *The Office* and movies like *Pirates of the Caribbean*. For the first time, the stage and all its stars could fit, not just in our homes, but in our pockets, traveling with us wherever we might venture.[41] *Celebrities* became an omnipresent *reality*.

Enter social media. The rise of this technology allowed media users to become content creators, able to broadcast their ideas and identities far and wide. While social media allowed established celebrities to maintain and expand their audiences, it also provided a platform for those seeking the spotlight. The move from theater to television brought the stage and its celebrities closer. The move from television to smartphones and social media gave us the ability to take the stage, to chase our vainglorious dreams. As Chris Martin puts it, "We used to be the audience. Now we're the audience and the act."[42] *Celebrity status* has become an omnipresent *hope*. "Come, let us make a name for ourselves."

## FROM VAINGLORY TO *SOLI DEO GLORIA*

Today, anyone with an iPhone can seek to slake the lust for recognition. Now more than ever, we must remember that the call of Christ is not "Come, make a name for yourself," but "Come,

---

40. Martin, *Wolf in Their Pockets*, 25.
41. Martin, *Wolf in Their Pockets*, 27.
42. Martin, *Wolf in Their Pockets*, 29.

deny yourself, and follow me."[43] The Christ-follower does not seek glory; rather, she glorifies God. He tattoos on his life that wonderful phrase, *soli Deo gloria*, "glory to God alone." It's not my glory story, but God's. To forsake vainglory is to give up on trying to be at the center of the universe, at the center of everyone's attention. It is to admit freely, from beginning to end, "It's not about me."[44] Does this mean that all forms of personal recognition are wrong? No. However, it does mean that any acknowledgment or applause we receive should be seen as an opportunity to lift high the ultimate source of our abilities, skills, or contributions. An author who claims another's words as his own is a plagiarist. A creature who claims to be the source of his or her own accomplishments is a cosmic plagiarist. Perhaps you *do* possess an impressive intellectual acumen or unparalleled rhetorical skills. But as God reminded Moses, "Who has made man's mouth?" (Exod 4:11). As mere creatures, any praise directed to us is akin to perfume: keep it on the surface and it's harmless; drink it into the heart and it becomes poisonous.

In Matt 6, Jesus warns us about doing good things in order to gain the attention of a crowd. "Beware of practicing your righteousness before other people in order to be seen by them," he says, "for then you will have no reward from your Father who is in heaven." He continues, "When you give to the needy, sound no trumpet before you, as the hypocrites do in the synagogues and in the streets, that they may be praised by others" (Matt 6:1–2). If Jesus had made this point in our technological moment, I wonder if he would have said, "When you give to the needy, post no updates on social"? If we want our virtue to go viral for our name's sake, then it's not true virtue, but the vice of vainglory masquerading as virtue.

What's particularly interesting about this passage is that it comes just one chapter after Jesus calls us to shine as the light of the world. In Matt 5:14–16, he says, "You are the light of the world. A city set on a hill cannot be hidden. Nor do people light a lamp

---

43. My paraphrase of Matt 16:24; Mark 8:34; Luke 9:23.
44. DeYoung, *Glittering Vices*, 53.

and put it under a basket, but on a stand, and it gives light to all in the house. In the same way, let your light shine before others, so that they may see your good works and give glory to your Father who is in heaven." Here, Jesus urges us to shine brightly, that is, *to be seen*, and to be seen by as many people as possible. How do we reconcile this with his admonition in Matt 6: "Sound no trumpet"? The final part of Matt 5:16 is the pivotal part: "Let your light shine before others, so that they may see your good works, *and give glory to your Father who is in heaven*." In this scenario, the attention is not on us, not on our virtue, but on God, the source of whatever good we display. To stick with Jesus' language, there are two ways to shine. I can shine like the sun, behaving as if I'm the blazing center, desiring everything to revolve around me. Or I can shine like the moon, simply reflecting the far greater light of Christ to the world.[45]

When the Christ-follower tattoos on his life *soli Deo gloria*, he does so with a restful heart. Why struggle to make a name for ourselves when already God has given us a name: child, image, and beloved? Our celebrity culture has made being visible to the masses the singular mark of success.[46] A person becomes a persona, then a brand, and finally an empire: glorious goal attained. But empires fall, just like Egypt. It's the public's judgment of celebrities that allows them to maintain their status. Celebrity is more accessible and producible than ever before, but the public remains fickle.[47] With his typical wit, Watkin warns, "Seeking to make a name for ourselves condemns us to a punishing regime of ever-inadequate performance, ever more forced and filtered self-presentation, and the ever-provisional, ever-changeable verdict of the social network

---

45. Martin, *Wolf in Their Pockets*, 107. Stephens and Deal, "God Who Gives Generously," 58, write, "Image-bearers are truly honoured when one sees through them to the one whose image they bear."

46. Douglas and McDonnell, *Celebrity*, 264.

47. Boorstin, *Image*, 63: "The very agency which first makes the celebrity in the long run destroys him. He will be destroyed, as he was made, by publicity. The newspapers make him, and they unmake him—not by murder but by suffocation or starvation. No one is more forgotten than the last generation's celebrity."

## VAINGLORY

on the name we have made for ourselves."[48] This makes me think of the way Ambrose Bierce defined the word *famous*: "conspicuously miserable."[49]

---

48. Watkin, *Biblical Critical Theory*, 213.
49. Bierce, *Devil's Dictionary*, 487.

# 3

# Envy

Seeing Everyone, Everywhere, All the Time

### THE FAIREST OF ALL THE FAIR

IN A FARAWAY COUNTRY there lived a beautiful queen with a fairy looking-glass. Regularly, the queen would go to the looking-glass, gaze upon herself, and inquire, "Tell me, glass, tell me true! Of all the ladies in the land, who is fairest, tell me, who?" Always, the glass had answered, "Thou, queen, art the fairest in all the land." But the young Snow White grew more and more beautiful, and by the time of her seventh birthday she had become as bright as the day and fairer than the queen herself. Thus, the looking-glass one day answered the queen, "Thou, queen, art fair, and beauteous to see, but Snow White is lovelier far than thee!" From that day forward, whenever the queen looked at Snow White, her heart heaved with hatred.

One day, the queen gave orders to a servant: "Take Snow White away into the wide wood, that I may never see her again." Thinking her vile work accomplished, the queen returned to her looking-glass with her usual query. But the magic of the glass was powerful; its gaze limitless. The glass answered, "Thou, queen, art the fairest in all *this* land. But over the hills, in the greenwood shade, where the seven dwarfs their dwelling have made, there

Snow White is hiding her head; and she is lovelier, far, O queen!" The queen knew that the glass spoke only truth, and she could not bear the thought of someone more beautiful than she, in this land or in any other. Thus, she disguised herself as a peasant's wife, traveled to the house of the dwarfs, and there she did the wicked deed herself: she poisoned her challenger.

When the queen returned to her kingdom and summoned her beloved glass, it uttered the words she most coveted: "Thou, queen. Thou art the fairest of all the fair." And at long last, her envious heart had rest—so far as an envious heart can . . . .[1]

The Grimm brothers' fairy tale popularized by Walt Disney is anything but a cartoonish or outlandish story. It's *real* and *present*. We need only to change a few details. In her beloved magical glass, the queen could both see herself and hear how she compared to others. The glass itself possessed the power to search the world, seeing everyone, everywhere, all the time. And in the queen's assessment, the glass was the definer of beauty, the giver of identity, the communicator of truth. Replace the evil queen and Snow White with Girl One and Girl Two, replace fairy looking-glass with iPhone and social media, and we no longer have an ancient tale set in a faraway country but a typical Friday in virtually every middle and high school. I'm beginning to think the Grimm brothers were prophets.

## BITTER TOWARD A BROTHER

The second capital vice, envy, is one of which Scripture speaks frequently, and always with the strongest of language. According to Prov 14:30, "A tranquil heart gives life to the flesh, but envy makes the bones rot."[2] A pungent description. That smell wafting through the nostrils is the slow rotting of the envious person. Envy eats away at both soul and body; it destroys one's mental, emotional,

---

1. My adaptation of the Brothers Grimm, *Snow White and Other Grimms' Fairy Tales*, 13–26.
2. "Bones" is a metonymy; the basic structure of the person signifies the person himself, who in this case is utterly destroyed.

and physical health. In the apostle Paul's famous description of love in 1 Cor 13, he helps us better understand love by telling us what it *does not do*, how it *does not behave*. What's first in Paul's list of negative statements? "Love does not envy" (1 Cor 13:4). Just before listing the fruit of the Spirit, Paul lists the works of the flesh: "sexual immorality, impurity, sensuality, idolatry, sorcery, enmity, strife, jealousy, fits of anger, rivalries, dissensions, divisions, envy, drunkenness, orgies, and things like these" (Gal 5:19–21a). "I warn you," he continues, "those who do such things will not inherit the kingdom of God" (v. 21b). For this reason, the apostle Peter calls us to "strip off" or to "put away" all envy (1 Pet 2:1).[3] To do this, however, we must push a bit further, to a more acute understanding of this vice and of how it creeps up on us.

In her book *Glittering Vices*, Rebecca Konyndyk DeYoung defines envy as "feeling bitter when others have it better."[4] She notes that, unlike covetousness and greed, which tend to focus on what we *have* or *own* ("stuff"), envy concentrates its concern on who we *are* ("status").[5] Envy's eye surveys the world, seeing the excellence or esteem of others as a personal insult. In Rom 12:15, Paul writes, "Rejoice with those who rejoice, weep with those who weep." "Weep with those who weep," that part most of us can muster. But "rejoice with those who rejoice," that part is much more difficult. Sure, I can weep when others are suffering, all the while giving thanks that it's not me who's suffering.[6] But how do I react when others are succeeding? What do I feel, think, and do when my friend gets the scholarship, the job, the promotion, the recognition, and I don't? It's the good news *for someone else* that can take us to the darkest of places.

---

3. The verb *apotithēmi* is used literally of dirty clothes being stripped from the body. Here it applies to filthy behaviors being stripped from the life.

4. DeYoung, *Glittering Vices*, 67.

5. DeYoung, *Glittering Vices*, 69.

6. I'm reminded of Tolstoy's words. News of Ivan's death "aroused in all who heard about it, as always, a feeling of delight that he had died, and they hadn't." Tolstoy, *Death of Ivan Ilyich and Other Stories*, 158.

A fictional story from the fourth century tells of novice demons finding great difficulty in tempting a monk. They sought to hook the godly man using every bait they had, but he couldn't be enticed. Frustrated, the novice demons returned to the devil and reported their failure. "Ah, your problem," the devil responded, "is that you've been far too *hard* on the monk. Send him a message that his brother has just been made bishop of Antioch. Bring him *good* news." Mystified by the devil's advice, the demons nevertheless went and did exactly as they were instructed. And in that very moment, when the good news arrived, the monk fell into deep, wicked envy.[7]

Envy has a tendency to escalate from thoughts and feelings to words and deeds, from secret and underhanded tactics to full-scale hatred and outright attack of a rival.[8] Like in the story of Snow White. Like in the story of Cain and Abel. The Bible contains some tragic chronicles of envy, and often among siblings.[9] The book of Genesis is the book of beginnings, of first things, including the first murder. In Gen 4:1–8, we read about the first two sons—Cain and Abel—born to the first man and woman—Adam and Eve:

> Now Adam knew Eve his wife, and she conceived and bore Cain, saying, "I have gotten a man with the help of the LORD." And again, she bore his brother Abel. Now Abel was a keeper of sheep, and Cain a worker of the ground. In the course of time Cain brought to the LORD an offering of the fruit of the ground, and Abel also brought of the firstborn of his flock and of their fat portions. And the LORD had regard for Abel and his offering, but for Cain and his offering he had no regard. So Cain was very angry, and his face fell. The LORD said to Cain, "Why are you angry, and why has your face fallen? If you do well, will you not be accepted? And if you do not do well, sin is crouching at the door. Its desire is for you, but you must rule over it." Cain spoke to Abel his

---

7. Hughes and Hughes, *Liberating Ministry from the Success Syndrome*, 100.

8. DeYoung, *Glittering Vices*, 72.

9. In addition to the example from Gen 4, see the Joseph narrative in Gen 37.

brother. And when they were in the field, Cain rose up against his brother Abel and killed him.

Immediately, the reader is struck by the celebratory scene at Cain's birth and the silence surrounding Abel's birth. When Cain arrives, Eve exudes gratitude: "I have gotten a man with the help of the LORD" (v. 1). When Abel arrives, Eve has no comment (v. 2). From the outset of the narrative, Cain seems to be the "somebody"; Abel the "nobody."[10] Abel plays a very small role in the chapter. He acts, but never speaks. He is present one moment and gone the next. Indeed, his name itself is an ominous foreshadowing; Abel means "vapor, breath."[11] Cain carries on his father's vocation as a servant of the ground (Gen 2:15). Abel is a keeper of flocks, a shepherd. Both are vocationally proficient, successful we might say. But which brother is the *most* successful?

Cain is the first man to bring an offering to God. As Tony Reinke puts it, "[Cain] owns the patent for the first human religious sacrifice, the enigmatic originator of the whole religious offering system."[12] Abel follows in big brother's footsteps. At first glance, each man's offering seems fitting enough, appropriate to his own occupation: Cain brings an offering from the ground; Abel brings an offering from his flock (vv. 3–4). But, to the reader's surprise, God receives Abel's offering and rejects Cain's. Why does God reject Cain? The answer lies in the details of v. 4: Abel brought "of the firstborn of his flock and of their fat portions." Miroslav Volf suggests that Cain, whose name means "to produce," was a wealthy farmer, a big landowner, whereas Abel was a simple man with just enough infertile land to keep a small flock. Cain the "great" brought a little something to God. Abel the "little," keenly aware of his dependence on God, brought a great offering, the best parts ("fat portions") of the best animals ("the firstborn of his flock").[13]

---

10. Volf, *Exclusion and Embrace*, 92.
11. Waltke, *Genesis*, 97.
12. Reinke, *God, Technology, and the Christian Life*, 82.
13. Volf, *Exclusion and Embrace*, 91. Similarly, Waltke, *Genesis*, 97, who concludes, "Cain's sin is tokenism. He looks religious, but in his heart he is not totally dependent on God, childlike, or grateful." Additionally, the writer

The good news of Abel's acclaim is too much for big brother to bear. How could Abel, who is clearly a "nobody," be regarded, while he, Cain, who is clearly a "somebody," be disregarded? From that day forward, whenever Cain looked at Abel, his heart heaved with hatred.

In the first premeditated murder, Cain waits patiently to be alone with Abel in some distant field. Perhaps he used one of his own farming tools as a weapon. Whatever the method, feelings about *self* because of comparison with *brother* grow into action *against brother*. Unable to restrain his resentment, Cain kills his own kin and leaves the body to be swallowed by the soil. It's poetic *in*justice. The very ground that previously seemed unproductive, that yielded no acclaim for Cain, now becomes his accomplice in the final swallowing and silencing of his rival. Following the murder comes the divine investigation, similar to the sequence involving Cain's parents in Gen 3. The first part of Cain's response is a lie. The second part is a rejection of God's question as an inappropriate one: "Am I my brother's keeper?" (v. 9). As God's role shifts from interrogator to prosecutor, again the reader is surprised by the narrative, this time by the sentence. Rather than being executed for his crime, Cain is *protected*. God marks Cain in some mysterious yet obvious way that says, "Don't mess with this guy."[14] We don't know exactly what this protective mark was or where it was placed, but it ensured for Cain a long life—though not the life of status and esteem he craved, not the life for which he took a life. Cain will be "a fugitive and a wanderer on the earth" (v. 12), a man marked by anxiety and vagrancy.

In the end, Cain gets what his envious heart desired: the removal of his rival-brother. But the tragic result is that he is now a man without community. By his envy, he excludes himself from all relationships. "No belonging is possible, only distance."[15] The

---

of Hebrews interprets this Old Testament story for us, indicating that Abel's offering was accepted because he trusted God in a way that Cain did not (Heb 11:4).

14. Reinke, *God, Technology, and the Christian Life*, 84.
15. Volf, *Exclusion and Embrace*, 95.

## Deathly (De)vices

passage concludes with Cain departing from the presence of the LORD and settling in the land of Nod, which means "wandering." DeYoung is right when she insists that "envy is a loser's game."[16] "Winning" at envy means destroying relationships, earning not a prize but a long life in the land of lostness and loneliness.

## OUR FAIRY LOOKING-GLASS

In the previous chapter, I provided a brief history of screens—from the theater to the smartphone. As the screens have become *smaller*, the stage has become *larger*. Anyone with an iPhone and social media can take the stage, so to speak. Here I want to expand on this idea, focusing on the development of social media. Recall the fairy tale with which this chapter began. In her magical glass, the queen could both see herself and discover how she compared to people far and wide. And in the queen's assessment, the glass, and *only* the glass, was the arbiter of all disputes about beauty. The smartphone loaded with selfie-based social media is our fairy looking-glass. As in the tale, we turn to this singular device to see our own reflections (or a carefully curated version of ourselves), for comparison, and for adjudication. This is true especially for those born in 1995 or later.

In *The Anxious Generation*, Jonathan Haidt tells the story of what happened to the generation born after 1995, commonly known as Gen Z or iGen, the generation that follows the Millennials (those born between 1981 and 1995).[17] What causes generations to differ goes beyond the events children experience, such as wars and depressions, and includes changes in the technologies they used during childhood.[18] The oldest members of iGen hit puberty around 2009, around the same time that four tech trends converged. The first two I've already mentioned: (1) the spread

---

16. DeYoung, *Glittering Vices*, 80.

17. The following discussion is based on Haidt, *Anxious Generation*, 1–45. Twenge prefers the designation iGen because this is the first generation for whom internet access has been constantly available. See Twenge, *iGen*, 1–16.

18. See Twenge, *Generations*.

of high-speed broadband in the 2000s, and (2) the arrival of the iPhone in 2007. (3) The third tech trend was a new age of digital interaction, which began in 2009 with the arrival of the "like" and "retweet" or "share" buttons. Haidt explains that before 2009, "social media was most useful as a way to keep up with your friends, and with fewer instant and reverberating feedback functions, it generated much less of the toxicity we see today."[19] (4) A fourth tech trend began just a few years later: the prevalence of posting selfies. The iPhone 4 was introduced in June 2010. It was the first iPhone with a front-facing camera, which made it much easier to capture photos or videos of oneself. That same year, Instagram was created as an app that could be used only on smartphones. Instagram had a smaller user base until 2012, when Facebook acquired it. Its user base then grew from ten million near the end of 2011 to ninety million by early 2013. Haidt concludes, "The smartphone and selfie-based social media ecosystem that we know today emerged in 2012, with Facebook's purchase of Instagram following the introduction of the front-facing camera. By 2012, many teen girls would have felt that 'everyone' was getting a smartphone and an Instagram account, and everyone was comparing themselves with everyone else."[20] Of course, this combined monopoly on the selfie market didn't last long. By mid 2015, Snapchat had more than one hundred million users. TikTok arrived in the United States in 2018 and surpassed the one-hundred-million mark within two years.[21]

On the most prototypical platforms, users first present a version of themselves (i.e., reflection). One of the most interesting questions to ponder is: Why do we present one version of ourselves instead of another?[22] Take a minute to look through the last dozen or so posts on your preferred platform. How do you decide

19. Haidt, *Anxious Generation*, 6.
20. Haidt, *Anxious Generation*, 35. On a related note, what is the purpose of Facebook? The company tells us the purpose is to "bring the world closer together." But Facebook began as a tool that Harvard students used to rate each other's physical attractiveness. Comparison is there at the origin of the thing. See Bail, *Breaking the Social Media Prism*, 128.
21. Bail, *Breaking the Social Media Prism*, 121.
22. Bail, *Breaking the Social Media Prism*, 48.

## Deathly (De)Vices

what should be included in this ever-expanding digital archive of your existence? More importantly, what do you *not* post on social media? What do you *not* reveal about yourself? After posting this carefully curated version of the self, the user waits for the judgment of the looking-glass (i.e., comparison and adjudication). With today's evolution of social media, status is quantifiable. The user has almost instant metrics to learn whether her presentation of self is winning the most acclaim. How many likes or shares do I have compared to her? How many followers or friends do I have compared to him? This technology enables us to compare ourselves to others with unprecedented scale and speed. When I was in high school, we changed classes every hour or so, and the hallway was the place where you saw everyone you knew, where comparison commenced, where envy set in. Social media platforms are the new high school hallways, and it feels like we never leave.[23]

Such constant comparison has proven detrimental, particularly for girls. In the early 2010s, both boys and girls started spending more time online, though they spent their time differently. Boys gravitated toward YouTube videos and online multiplayer video games. Girls became much heavier users of the new visually oriented platforms like Instagram.[24] Dozens of experiments conducted by leading social psychologists have led to the same conclusion: Social media is a cause of anxiety, depression, and other ailments.[25] Megan Armstrong, a University of Missouri student who struggles with depression, says, "You're constantly hearing about what this person did that was really awesome. It always makes me wonder, what am I doing? What should I be doing? Is it enough?"[26] At age nineteen, Essena O'Neil, a model who made her living by posting her photos on Instagram, suddenly shut down her social media accounts. She later posted a YouTube video explaining the decision: "I spent hours watching perfect girls online, wishing I was

---

23. Thompson, *Hit Makers*, 159.

24. See the insightful discussion of why social media harms girls more than boys in Haidt, *Anxious Generation*, 143–72.

25. Haidt, *Anxious Generation*, 148. See also Twenge, *iGen*, 93–118.

26. Twenge, *iGen*, 101.

them. Then, when I was 'one of them,' I still wasn't happy, content, or at peace with myself."[27] Haidt puts it in haunting terms: "This is the great irony of *social* media: the more you immerse yourself in it, the more *lonely* and *depressed* you become."[28] Like Cain, whose envy in the end excluded him from all relationships, those who make their home in this smartphone and selfie-based social media ecosystem eventually will discover that they have chosen life in the land of lostness and loneliness.

Pew Research finds that a third of today's teenagers confess to being on one of the major social media platforms "almost constantly."[29] And when they're not on their phones, their social and communication apps are vying for their attention. The average number of notifications on young people's phones amounts to nearly two hundred alerts per day. The average teen, who gets only seven hours of sleep per night, therefore gets eleven or twelve notifications per waking hour.[30] The queen had to summon her magic glass. Our glass summons us every five minutes![31] This makes it harder than ever to strip off all envy (1 Pet 2:1).

When writer Andy Crouch (author of *The Tech-Wise Family*, a book I highly recommend to parents and grandparents) took forty days offline—no screens of any kind—he said the fast from tech was mostly freeing and delightful, with one caveat:

> But I will say this: FOMO—the "fear of missing out"—is a real thing. What I was most afraid of missing out on was not information, but affirmation. I discovered how attached, or maybe addicted, I was to the small daily dose of reassurance that other people "like" me and "follow" me.... It was sobering how strong the pull was on me.[32]

27. Twenge, *iGen*, 106.
28. Haidt, *Anxious Generation*, 179 (emphasis added).
29. Haidt, *Anxious Generation*, 119.
30. Haidt, *Anxious Generation*, 126.
31. Reinke, *12 Ways Your Phone Is Changing You*, 16, says we now check our smartphones every 4.3 minutes of our waking lives. Compare Turkle, *Reclaiming Conversation*, 42, who says the average American adult checks his or her phone every six and a half minutes.
32. Cited in Reinke, *12 Ways Your Phone Is Changing You*, 156.

# Deathly (De)Vices

Many of us can relate to Crouch's struggle. Though I wonder if by giving it this innocuous acronym—FOMO—we lose sight of what it truly is. FOMO is an alias, a cover-up for envy. What's at the core of FOMO? Comparison. FOMO is the fear of missing out on what someone else is experiencing. Cain had FOMO in relation to Abel: he feared missing out on the commendation his brother received. The queen had FOMO with respect to Snow White: she feared missing out on the beauty this young girl possessed. Where there is no comparison, there can be no FOMO. It takes at least *two* for FOMO to exist. It takes at least *two* to envy. But not just any two.

When I was on social media, I followed people with whom I had common ground or common interests. Pastors, authors, CrossFitters. The problem is: These are the types of people I tend to envy. When I hear someone play beautiful music, I don't envy the artist, because I know that's not my gift. But when I hear a pastor give a great sermon, or learn of an author publishing another book, the flame of envy is ignited within me. Why? Because those are *my gifts*, and in my flesh, I want to be *the most gifted*. If you're a marketer, my hunch is you follow other marketers. If you're an artist, I'll bet you follow other artists. We populate our digital communities with the very people we are most likely to envy.

## A BETTER STORY

So, here many of us find ourselves: staring into a glass that allows us to see far more people than any civilization ever before has seen,[33] seeing especially the very people we are most inclined to envy, being summoned regularly to check our numbers, since they, and *only* they, are the arbiter of all disputes about status, and increasing evidence that an existence in this social media ecosystem leads to Nod—anxiety and vagrancy, lostness and loneliness. What, then, are we to do? Psychologist Jean Twenge suggests, "There is a simple,

---

33. The deeper I reflect on it, the more convinced I am that this is an adverse innovation. For good reason, God gave us eyes that see only so far, only so much. Rightly understood, our limits are a gift, not a deficiency. See Kapic, *You're Only Human*.

free way to improve mental health: put down the phone, and do something else."³⁴ Agreed. Though our digital resistance, like all spiritual disciplines, must be motivated ultimately by divine grace.

The basic storyline of the gospel—creation, fall, and redemption—reinvents the looking-glass concepts of reflection, comparison, and adjudication. Consider, first, the doctrine of creation. Prior to the episode of Cain and Abel, we hear the pronouncement of God: "Let us make man in our image, after our likeness" (Gen 1:26). Christopher Watkin notes the importance of both parts of the phrase: humanity is made "in the image" and "of God." "In the image" reminds us that we are indeed reflections, though of another. Understanding that we are created "in the image" will keep us from thinking too highly of ourselves and from attempting to achieve our own identity or status. Adam and Eve did not build the status of reflection by any of their own efforts. It was a gift given to them—and to us. The second part of the phrase, "of God," keeps us from thinking too little of ourselves. As Watkin so eloquently puts it, "A murmuration of migrating martins is not in the image of God, nor is a breathtaking beach, a rainforest, a radiant sunset, or a raging waterfall. Only one creature in the vast cornucopia of creation's diversity is dignified with this honor: you, me, and every human being from the richest and grandest to the poorest and lowliest."³⁵

Created in the image of God, designed to dwell in intimate fellowship with our Maker and to showcase his love, humanity rejected God, acted as our own gods; and for this rejection we deserve eternal separation from the loving and life-giving presence of our true Lord. But, the gospel declares, "while we were still sinners, Christ died for us" (Rom 5:8). The doctrine of the fall means that all are equally unworthy of God's love. The doctrine of redemption means that all who with faith look to Christ are equal recipients of God's grace. The eye of comparison has been gouged with a cruciform sword.

---

34. Twenge, *iGen*, 118.
35. Watkin, *Biblical Critical Theory*, 93.

Tony Reinke shares an illuminating story from one of his family vacations.[36] One day, while he and his teenage son were hiking, they found a beautiful waterfall. It was such a perfect spot that they decided to spend the day there. As midday arrived, and the sun's heat with it, Reinke's son asked if he could climb to the top of the waterfall and jump into the pond below. "Absolutely not," his father told him. "The water is too dark. We can't see what lies below the surface. You'll break your neck."[37] Later that afternoon, two road workers approached the edge of the cliff. Covered in asphalt, they stripped down to their shorts and leaped from the top of the waterfall, landing safely in the pond below. Then they climbed back to the top of the cliff and did it again. Reinke's son witnessed the whole thing, so he returned to his father, saying, "Dad, now we know it's safe! Can I jump?" As Reinke relays the story, he confesses that he could feel a sermon illustration being born in this very moment. He decided to give his son permission to jump, but with one condition. "No one can video it," he said. "Jump and enjoy the thrill of it. But no one can post it on social media for others to see." Immediately, his son threw up his arms and protested, "Then what's the point?!"

Not just our teenage children, but all of us, desperately want to be seen. We want to do something that will grab the attention of others. Jump off the waterfall or whatever it takes. The desire is ingrained within us. The message of the gospel is simply this: *God sees you.* You don't have to do something spectacular to grab his attention. He's already done something spectacular to demonstrate just how much you have his attention, his affection: "while we were still sinners, Christ died for us" (Rom 5:8). The word of adjudication has been heard.

I've always loved the section of *The Westminster Confession* that explains faith: "Faith, thus receiving and resting on Christ and his righteousness, is the alone instrument of justification: yet is it not alone in the person justified, but is ever accompanied with all

---

36. DeYoung, "Technology Is Neither Good, nor Bad, nor Neutral with Tony Reinke and Samuel James."

37. My paraphrase of Reinke.

other saving graces, and is no dead faith, but worketh by love."[38] In other words, receiving and resting in Christ awakens us to a whole new way of living. It frees us from the idea that we can show only certain versions of ourselves, the most pleasant and polished forms. The Christian practice of confession of sin subverts the social media mechanism with its clarion call for curation. In confession, we abandon airbrushing; we bare all before God, with the confidence that—because of Jesus' death and resurrection—God knows us all the way to the bottom *and* loves us all the way to the skies. On his or her best day and worst day, the believer is the beloved of God. Grasping this reality is the first step in quelling whatever bitterness I have toward my brother. When I envy, I can only love myself if I find myself the better man. In the story of Cain and Abel, it was Cain's feelings about *himself* that caused him to slay his sibling. The command is to love my *neighbor* as I love *myself* (Matt 22:39). With the eye of envy, I can do neither.[39] With heart and eyes that rest in the gospel of grace, I can do both.

---

38. *Westminster Confession of Faith* 11.2, in Dixhoorn, *Confessing the Faith*.
39. DeYoung, *Glittering Vices*, 79.

# 4

# Sloth

Being Lazy at Love

### DON'T GET HIGH ON YOUR OWN SUPPLY

AT AN APPLE EVENT in January 2010, Steve Jobs unveiled the iPad.[1] For ninety minutes, Jobs explained why this new device would surpass the laptop. He believed everyone should own an iPad. Everyone except his children. In late 2010, he told *New York Times* journalist Nick Bilton that his children had never used the iPad. "We limit how much technology our kids use in the home," Jobs said. Bilton discovered that several other tech giants established similar boundaries. Chris Anderson, former editor of *Wired*, enforced strict time limits on every device in his home. His five children were not allowed to use screens in their bedrooms. Lesley Gold, the founder of an analytics company, had a strict no-screens-during-the-week rule for her children. Walter Isaacson, who wrote a bestselling biography of Steve Jobs, says that while eating dinner with the Jobs family he never saw anyone use an Apple product. "The kids did not seem addicted at all to devices."

---

1. The following account, including quotes from Steve Jobs and Walter Isaacson, comes from Alter, *Irresistible*, 1–3.

# Sloth

Evidently, the creators of tech products follow the cardinal rule of drug dealing: Don't get high on your own supply.[2]

Some of the world's greatest technocrats are also some of the greatest technophobes. They, better than anyone, know the addictive power of their creations. Instagram is bottomless. Facebook has an endless feed. Netflix automatically moves on to the next episode. For companies like Netflix to grow their bottom lines, people must binge-watch more. In tech parlance, it's all about "engagement," minutes and hours of eyeballs on the product.[3] The longer we look at their product, the more advertising we see, and the more money these companies get. And how do they accomplish this goal? Everything we do online is tracked. "Over time, the history of every like, pin, email, swipe, and hashtag creates your epic digital biography."[4] This biography feeds algorithms, "recommendation engines" designed to deliver optimally interesting content to maximize our time on platform, to keep us engaged.[5] Streaming services like Netflix, Amazon, and YouTube can accurately predict what you're most likely to watch next, because they know everything else you've ever watched, and they know what people like you have watched next. They have everything they need to keep us watching, and watching, and watching—into oblivion.

## THE LIGHTWEIGHT VICE AND THE HEAVIEST COMMANDMENTS

The third vice—sloth—probably is the least thought about of the seven, and when it is thought about, likely it's pictured as the lightweight of the group.[6] We've seen that envy led to the first murder.

---

2. Alter, *Irresistible*, 2. See also Turkle, *Reclaiming Conversation*, 55, who reports that Silicon Valley parents who work for social media companies often send their children to technology-free schools with the hope that this will give their children greater emotional and intellectual range.

3. Hari, *Stolen Focus*, 113.

4. Smith, *(Un)Intentional*, 17. See also Hari, *Stolen Focus*, 105–42.

5. Martin, *Wolf in Their Pockets*, 45.

6. Willimon, *Sinning Like a Christian*, 76.

# Deathly (De)Vices

It's equally effortless to imagine how avarice or wrath might ruin someone's life. But sloth seems less sinister, less serious. What's the worst that could come from lying in bed a bit too long, binge-watching our favorite shows or scrolling on social media? Does little old sloth really belong in this list of capital vices, among such bad company?

In the book of Proverbs, we find certain recurring characters. The forbidden woman is one such character. Another is the sluggard, a figure of both comedy and tragedy.[7] The author of Proverbs wants us to laugh at the absurdity of the sluggard and to learn from his tragic mistakes, thereby avoiding these blunders ourselves. "The sluggard does not plow in the autumn; he will seek at harvest and have nothing" (Prov 20:4). "The sluggard says, 'There is a lion outside! I shall be killed in the streets'" (Prov 22:13). "As a door turns on its hinges, so does a sluggard on his bed. [He] buries his hand in the dish; it wears him out to bring it back to his mouth" (Prov 26:14–15). The sluggard fails to plan for *tomorrow*. He makes excuses so he won't have to face the responsibilities of *today*. He *wastes the day* by staying in bed. Indeed, his habitual inactivity makes something so basic as eating a bowl of Cheerios seem like work. By inches and minutes, the sluggard's life slips away. Too many refusals, and too many postponements. And "it has all been as imperceptible, and as pleasant, as falling asleep."[8]

This tragicomic character surfaces as often as he does in Proverbs because laziness is more than a minor character flaw; it's a serious spiritual problem. At times, I remind my sons of the two things I despise more than anything else: laziness and lying. Why do I find these behaviors particularly abhorring? Because lying breaks the relationships God has given us, and laziness wastes the talents God has given us. God is the Creator of all things, the Giver of all good gifts, including the people in your life, your capacities and opportunities, and your life's ultimate purpose. From the perspective of Christian theology, then, sloth is a disregard for God

---

7. See the discussion in Kidner, *Proverbs*, 39–40.
8. Kidner, *Proverbs*, 40.

## Sloth

as Giver, a wasteful response to his abundant blessings, an apathy toward our kingdom calling.[9]

A scene in *The Last Jedi* (the most controversial film in the *Star Wars* saga, I know) illustrates this point forcefully (pun intended).[10] When finally Rey finds Luke Skywalker on his island sanctuary on the planet Ahch-To, she hands him the lightsaber. Rey's simple gesture speaks volumes: it communicates, "Luke, you have a unique gift. You have a profound calling." Luke grasps the lightsaber, gazes at it for a second or two, and then tosses it over his shoulder and off the cliff. That's sloth—in Jedi form. In ordinary human form, sloth grasps our God-given strengths, place, and purpose, tosses the whole bundle over our shoulder, and climbs back in bed for another episode of *Stranger Things* or *Cobra Kai*. "Sloth opposes the great Christian virtue of diligence—that powerful sense of responsibility, dedication to hard work, and conscientious completion of our God-given duties."[11] The root of the English word *diligence* is the Latin *diligere*, which means "to love." To see sloth's true colors, we must see the resistance to love that lies behind it.

Turning from the OT to the NT, we find an exchange between Jesus and an expert in the law that crystallizes the severity of this third vice. Sloth can't be considered the lightweight of the capital vices, because it violates the *heaviest* or *greatest* commandments:

> But when the Pharisees heard that [Jesus] had silenced the Sadducees, they gathered together. And one of them, a lawyer, asked him a question to test him. "Teacher, which is the great commandment in the Law?" And he said to him, "You shall love the Lord your God with all your heart and with all your soul and with all your mind. This is the great and first commandment. And a second is like it: You shall love your neighbor as yourself. On

---

9. DeYoung, *Glittering Vices*, 92; Willimon, *Sinning Like a Christian*, 83.
10. Johnson, *Last Jedi*.
11. DeYoung, *Glittering Vices*, 89.

## Deathly (De)Vices

these two commandments depend all the Law and the Prophets." (Matt 22:34–40)[12]

Jesus regularly came into conflict with the religious establishment, especially the Pharisees, who feared that he was destroying the very basis of their divinely established religion. In this case, a spokesman of the Pharisees, one who is described as being especially learned in the law of Moses, approaches Jesus with a question. The question itself seems harmless, but Matthew comments on the lawyer's intent: His purpose is to test Jesus, that is, to trick him into saying something that will discredit him. This is not simply an academic exercise.

The question is, "Teacher, which is the great commandment in the Law?" (v. 36). The rabbis divided the commandments into the "light" and the "heavy." This didn't mean that some commandments were so light that they could be ignored. All the commandments were from God; therefore, all were to be obeyed. However, since the five books of Moses contained, by rabbinic calculation, 613 commandments, some means of assessing their relative weight was widely appreciated.[13] This lawyer wants to know which *one* commandment is *the weightiest*, the greatest of them all.

Though he is asked for but one commandment, Jesus gives two, as if to say that this is a package deal. The greatest commandment, he replies, is this: "You shall love the Lord your God with all your heart and with all your soul and with all your mind" (v. 37). Jesus quotes the beginning of the Shema, recorded in Deut 6:4–5. *Shema* is the first Hebrew word of the summons. "Shema, O Israel." "*Hear*, O Israel: The LORD our God, the LORD is one."[14] There is but one true God,[15] and there is but one fitting response to this God, which Jesus cites here in Matt 22. The combination of

---

12. See also Mark 12:28–31; Luke 10:25–28.
13. France, *Gospel of Matthew*, 842.
14. Jesus could hardly have chosen a more familiar text. The Shema was recited every morning and every evening. It outlined the spiritual formation of God's OT people: memorize, recite, teach, write, and even wear God's word.
15. Wright, *Deuteronomy*, 96, notes that the verse can be read in terms of Yahweh's incomparability, his singularity, or his integrity.

terms—*heart, soul,* and *mind*—and the repetition of the word *all* emphasize that this allegiance to the one true God stems from the deepest part of us and involves the complete surrender of the life.[16]

To this, Jesus adds, "You shall love your neighbor as yourself" (v. 39).[17] The person who loves God wholeheartedly will increasingly see others the way God sees them and love them the way he loves them. The apostle John makes no bones about it: "If anyone says, 'I love God,' and hates his brother, he is a liar; for he who does not love his brother whom he has seen cannot love God whom he has not seen. And this commandment we have from him: whoever loves God must also love his brother" (1 John 4:20–21). When Jesus speaks of loving our "neighbor," he means more than the person with a property adjacent to ours. For Jesus, there is no such thing as a *non-neighbor,* no type of person from whom his followers safely can withhold love.[18] However, we must be careful not to blunt the commandment by giving it an ambiguous object. It's much easier for me to feel that I'm successfully loving my neighbor, so long as "neighbor" remains an abstract term. Loving that objectionable person next door who is all too concrete a reality, that requires a much larger measure of Spirit-empowered human effort.[19] Stanley Hauerwas says, "To be a Christian is to be called to a life of love, but that calling is a lifelong task that requires our willingness to be surprised by what love turns out to be."[20] As it turns out, love is *work.* And work means being awake—awake to real people in the real world.

---

16. Mark 12:30 has four nouns (heart, life, mind, strength). The Septuagint has three (heart, life, strength). Morris, *Gospel According to Matthew,* 563, notes that we should not make too much of the difference, for each way of expressing it makes the point that we should love God with all that we *are* and all that we *have.*

17. A commandment contained in Lev 19:18, 34.

18. See the parable in Luke 10:25–37.

19. Morris, *Gospel According to Matthew,* 564.

20. Hauerwas, *Matthew,* 194.

Deathly (De)Vices

## HOW OUR TECHNOLOGIES HOOK US

Christopher Nolan's film *Inception* is an insightful parable about our relationship with technology.[21] *Inception* tells the story of a technology known as dream-sharing that allows participants to enter into one another's dreams via their subconscious. The protagonist is a dream hacker named Cobb, played by Leonardo DiCaprio. Cobb is especially skilled at entering into people's dreams and navigating their subconscious in order to find their most protected secrets. A billionaire CEO acquires Cobb's services, directing him to occupy the mind of a rival captain of industry and plant the idea of breaking up his company. As the film progresses and Cobb assembles his team of hackers, the viewer learns that dream-sharing is more than a technology for storming someone else's mind; it's also a way to build one's own subconscious reality. In one of the more disturbing scenes, Cobb's team visits a chemist who can concoct particularly potent sedatives which enable prolonged dream-sharing. The chemist leads Cobb's team downstairs to a dark room where dozens of men are sleeping, connected to his dream-sharing devices. He goes on to explain that these men come to his shop regularly and employ his sedative to dream together for hours and hours, constructing an alternative life in their dreams. Shocked by the sight, Cobb's team inquires, "They come here to fall asleep?" "No," the chemist responds. "They come here to wake up. The dream has become their reality. Who are you to say otherwise."

Dream-sharing is a fictitious technology (at least for now), but as Samuel James points out, "The near limitless ability to construct our own version of reality lies in our pockets or on our desks nearly every day. Much like the pitiable patients in the film, our relationship with these technologies has a way of causing us to desire digital sleep. As much as we might tell ourselves that we go to the internet and social media to be plugged into what's going on in the world, many times we're logging on to escape it."[22]

---

21. Nolan, *Inception*. I'm grateful to Samuel James for planting this analogy in my mind. See James, *Digital Liturgies*, 33–35.

22. James, *Digital Liturgies*, 34–35.

In his 2017 book, *Irresistible: The Rise of Addictive Technology and the Business of Keeping Us Hooked*, Adam Alter tells the story of an app developer named Kevin Holesh. Holesh decided that he wasn't spending enough time with his family. The culprit was technology. Curious about exactly how much time each day he was devoting to his devices, Holesh did what app developers do: he designed an app called Moment. Moment tracked Holesh's screen time, tallying how long he used his phone for internet-related tasks. Holesh discovered that he was spending an hour and fifteen minutes a day on his phone. Intrigued by the app, Alter himself decided to give it a try, guessing that he was devoting roughly an hour a day to his devices. Like most people, Alter's guess was entirely too low. After a month of monitoring, Moment reported that he was using his phone an average of three hours per day. Alter contacted Holesh to find out if his usage was typical. "Absolutely," Holesh replied. "We have thousands of users, and their average usage time is just under three hours."[23] Holesh then reminded Alter that these are people who care enough about their screen time to download a tracking app in the first place. Millions of smartphone users are oblivious, likely spending far more than three hours a day on their devices. At first blush, three hours might not sound too bad. But do the math. That's almost one hundred hours a month lost to surfing the web, scrolling on social media, checking email, texting, and so on. Over the average lifetime, that amounts to an astonishing *eleven years*.[24] Brett McCracken, author of *The Wisdom Pyramid*, admits, "When I find myself meandering on my phone—scrolling through Instagram, clicking random links, checking sports scores, or whatever—I often feel removed from my body, lost in a digital rabbit hole."[25] What if all that time in the digital rabbit hole added up to eleven years of your life? A sobering thought. When on the final day we answer to the Lord, our social media accounts and text

---

23. Alter, *Irresistible*, 14.

24. Alter, *Irresistible*, 15.

25. McCracken, *Wisdom Pyramid*, 16. Similarly, Turkle, *Reclaiming Conversation*, 13, writes, "Technology enchants; it makes us forget what we know about life."

# Deathly (De)Vices

message history will be the definitive evidence that our prayerlessness was not from lack of time.

There's both a science and an art behind the addictive nature of our technologies.[26] When an action is followed by a good outcome—grabbing a snack or relieving pain—certain brain circuits involved in learning release a bit of dopamine, the neurotransmitter centrally involved with feelings of pleasure and pain. The release of dopamine feels good, but not in a "that was nice; that's enough" sort of way. It's more like, "that was nice; now for more!" When you eat a potato chip, a piece of popcorn, or an M&M, you get a small hit of dopamine, which is why you reach for a second one. This is the same sensation one gets when playing slot machines. A win feels great, but usually it doesn't motivate the winner to take his money and go home; rather, the pleasure of the win leads him to continue gambling. It's the same for video games, social media, and other apps that cause people to spend far more time than they had intended to spend. And make no mistake: this is by design. "The creators of these apps use every trick in the psychologists' tool kit to hook users as deeply as slot machines hook gamblers."[27]

App designers commonly employ a four-step process that creates a self-perpetuating loop. This is sometimes referred to as the Hook Model, named after Nir Eyal's 2014 book, *Hooked: How to Build Habit-Forming Products*. In Eyal's own words, "Through consecutive Hook cycles, successful products reach their ultimate goal of unprompted user engagement, bringing users back repeatedly, without depending on costly advertising or aggressive messaging."[28] The process begins with an external *trigger*, such as a notification that someone has commented on one of my posts. The trigger is the off-ramp, enticing me to leave one road for another. The second step is the *action*, touching the notification, which takes me down the road of Instagram. The action produces a pleasurable outcome, but not always, which is the third step: *variable*

---

26. See, for example, Haidt, *Anxious Generation*, 129–36; Hari, *Stolen Focus*, 105–42; Song, *Restless Devices*, 39–61.

27. Haidt, *Anxious Generation*, 130.

28. Eyal, *Hooked*, 5.

## Sloth

*reward*. Eyal explains that what distinguishes the Hook Model is its ability to create craving. "The unsurprising response of your fridge light turning on when you open the door doesn't drive you to keep opening it again and again," he says. "However, add some variability to the mix—suppose a different treat magically appears in your fridge every time you open it—and *voilà*, intrigue is created."[29] Having turned down the road of Instagram, I may find an expression of praise, but maybe not. If not, I can always wander down the bottomless feed, enjoying the assortment of treats that magically appear there.

The fourth step of the Hook Model is *investment*. This final phase increases the odds that the user will make another pass through the cycle. Investment occurs when I put a little more of myself into the app. Already, I've established a profile, posted a number of selfies, and populated my digital community. But maybe I need to post a more interesting, more controversial photo. Maybe I need to accumulate a few more followers. Perhaps that's why I *didn't* get that expression of praise before. So, I post a more extreme picture, and I follow a handful of new people, hoping they'll reciprocate. At this point, after investment, the trigger may become *internal*, rather than *external*. I no longer require a notification to summon me to Instagram. While reading a book or sitting with my family, suddenly the thought forms in my mind, "I wonder if anyone has commented on that photo I posted earlier today."[30] And back to Instagram I go. Now, I'm hooked. No wonder Jobs and other tech industry leaders swore off many of their own technologies. It's the makers of a bomb who best understand its destructive potential.

Whereas girls are more likely to become hooked on social media,[31] boys are more apt to abandon the real world for the

---

29. Eyal, *Hooked*, 8.

30. Song, *Restless Devices*, 54, is spot on: "The special sauce of the Instagrams, Snapchats, and Twitters of this world is a built-in feedback mechanism that preys on our human desire for quantifiable and repeated peer acknowledgment and affirmation." Hari, *Stolen Focus*, 115, speaks of the "treadmill of continuous checking."

31. I address this point in the previous chapter.

## Deathly (De)Vices

virtual world of video games.³² The story of gaming begins in the 1970s with arcade games like *Pong*. As a kid growing up in the '80s, I remember playing games like *Frogger* and *Q-Bert* on my dad's Atari. In those days, I don't think anyone talked about boys being addicted to video games. If you spend a few minutes playing *Q-Bert*, you'll understand why. In the 1990s, new video game technologies emerged, including first-person shooter games like *Doom*, and later, multiplayer online games like *World of Warcraft*. "These internet-connected consoles enabled adolescents to sit alone in a room, playing for extended hours with a shifting set of strangers from around the globe. Prior to this, when boys played multiplayer video games, the other players were their friends or their siblings, sitting next to them and sharing excitement, jokes, and food."³³ At the same time that games became faster, brighter, better, overall more immersive, the gaming experience became more sequestered, removed from flesh-and-blood people. For many boys, the virtual world became the *preferred* world. Addicted gamers often conceal their gaming use, lose interest in real-world activities, withdraw from family and friends, and use gaming as a means of psychological escape.³⁴ These boys have become like the men from *Inception*, hidden in the basement, connected to their devices. The game has become their reality.

## THE DREAM OF THE SORCERERS' APPRENTICE

One of my literary heroes is J. R. R. Tolkien, who has wrongly been thought an utter technophobe.³⁵ A closer reading of Tolkien's life and characters reveals, not an irrational, curmudgeonly dismissal of all technology but a sagacious concern about the limits and

---

32. See the discussion in Haidt, *Anxious Generation*, 173–97.

33. Haidt, *Anxious Generation*, 185.

34. Haidt, *Anxious Generation*, 191, finds that one out of every thirteen adolescent boys suffers from substantial impairment in the real world because of heavy engagement with video games.

35. Ordway, *Tolkien's Modern Reading*, 203–7, provides a well-articulated correction to this view.

proper uses of technological innovations.³⁶ In *The Hobbit*, Tolkien introduces goblins as creatures who "make no beautiful things, but they make many clever ones . . . . Hammers, axes, swords, daggers, pickaxes, tongs, and also instruments of torture, they make very well, or get other people to make to their design, prisoners and slaves that have to work till they die." He continues, "It is not unlikely that [goblins] invented some of the machines that have since troubled the world, especially the ingenious devices for killing large numbers of people at once, for wheels and engines and explosions always delighted them, and also not working with their own hands more than they could help."³⁷ For Tolkien, the evil of goblin tech is associated with its utility: It is a means of dominating the will of another and a means of avoiding work.³⁸

Contrary to goblins, Hobbits take joy in the work of their hands; they wield tools. "[Hobbits] love peace and quiet and good tilled earth: a well-ordered and well-farmed countryside was their favorite haunt. They do not and did not understand or like machines more complicated than a forge-bellows, a water-mill, or a hand-loom."³⁹ Tools multiply force. And the force that most tools multiplied until very recently in human history came from bodies, either the bodies of domesticated animals or the bodies of human beings. In the modern era, we found new sources of power, all of which derive from combustion, fission, or fusion. In his illuminating essay "The Alchemists' Dream," Andy Crouch remarks, "All the power available to us traces its way back, you might say only slightly hyperbolically, to explosions."⁴⁰ In addition to harnessing power

---

36. Tolkien's writing includes a story about an eccentric man who buys a motor car (*Mr. Bliss*). In an interview with the BBC, Tolkien even declared that he loved motor cars: "Love riding in them, like driving them." When asked for more details, he explained that the problem is not the automobile itself, but the number of them: "Anything that's good in one or two is nearly always bad at 5,000." Cited in Ordway, *Tolkien's Modern Reading*, 205.

37. Tolkien, *Hobbit*, 59.

38. Dickerson, "Wendell Berry, C. S. Lewis, J. R. R. Tolkien and the Dangers of a Technological Mindset."

39. Tolkien, *Fellowship of the Ring*, 10.

40. Crouch, "Alchemists' Dream," 38.

in a novel way, at the dawn of the technological era we created what came to be known as cybernetic systems, eventually enabling autonomous and automatic operation. With these two interdependent developments, we were able to achieve what Crouch calls "the dream of the Sorcerer's Apprentice: things that work on their own, no bodies or minds directly required."[41] In Walt Disney's 1940 film *Fantasia*, the apprentice succeeds in getting the broom to work autonomously, but we all know how that played out. "Easy everything"—this seems to be the motto of much of today's tech. What developers want, unlike what the old toolmakers wanted, is not to *extend* human engagement with the world, but to *replace* human engagements. They, and at times *we*, want tech to take over for us. Crouch says there are two fundamental promises made on behalf of every device. The first is "now you'll be able to . . ." and the second is "you'll no longer have to . . . ." In our time, the balance has shifted to the latter promise. "Our main fascination with technology is not the things it enables us to do, but the things we no longer have to do."[42]

But, as Crouch goes on to point out, there are two additional realties of technology that are less often considered, chiefly because they don't drive sales. The inevitable correlates of "now you'll be able to . . ." and "you'll no longer have to . . ." are *"you'll no longer be able to . . ."* and *"now you'll have to . . . ."* "Technology does not just expand what 'we' (our devices acting on our behalf) can do—it also removes capacity and enforces new behaviors."[43] For example, in the modern era we've replaced the hearth, the source of heat and light that for thousands of years was at the center of human dwellings, with the furnace, controlled by a thermostat. *Now you'll be able to* keep the temperature of your home precisely at seventy-two degrees; and *you'll no longer have to* venture outside to find firewood. But *you'll no longer be able to* gather around a fire that illuminates, offers warmth, and draws people from the edges of the home. You've gained comfort but sacrificed the center of the

---

41. Crouch, "Alchemists' Dream," 38–39.
42. Crouch, "Alchemists' Dream," 41.
43. Crouch, "Alchemists' Dream," 42.

home. Technology giveth, and technology taketh away. "The trade of the hearth for the furnace," Crouch writes, "was one large step toward the reality of modern middle-class American home life, where many members of the household much of the time are alone in their bedrooms, engaged with glowing rectangles, rather than gathered at the center in community around the primal, mysterious . . . glow of the fire."[44]

## WORK WORTH DOING

Many of our technologies tempt us toward escapism and easy-everything existence. Only a reverberant and full-orbed proclamation of the gospel can silence sloth's whisper. The gospel declaration involves a transformation in the way we *work*. Experiencing the love *of* God and expressing love *for* God necessarily prompts love *for* neighbor. "You were dead in [your] trespasses and sins," Paul writes. "But God, being rich in mercy, because of the great love with which he loved us, even when we were dead in our trespasses, made us alive together with Christ." We are now "his workmanship, created in Christ Jesus *for good works*, which God prepared beforehand, that we should walk in them" (Eph 2:1, 4–5, 10). We are saved by grace, but true grace is transformative grace: it changes us. We are saved by grace through faith, but true faith has feet: it walks in the real world; it does works of love for real people.

The work with which to begin, it seems to me, is the work of *seeing our fellow humans*. It's been said that in the digital era, love is a lack of desire to check one's iPhone in another's presence.[45] Somewhere along the way, we lost the power to lock eyes with another human being. Sherry Turkle highlights that most people would rather send an email or text message than commit to a phone call or face-to-face conversation. "This new mediated life has gotten us into trouble. Face-to-face conversation is the most human—and humanizing—thing we do. Fully present to one

---

44. Crouch, "Alchemists' Dream," 44.
45. Turkle, *Reclaiming Conversation*, 177, citing Alain De Botton.

## Deathly (De)Vices

another, we learn to listen. It's where we develop the capacity for empathy."[46] Turkle draws on the work of psychiatrist Daniel Siegel, arguing that children need eye contact to develop the parts of the brain involved with attachment. "Repeated tens of thousands of times in the child's life, these small moments of mutual rapport [serve to] transmit the best part of our humanity—our capacity for love—from one generation to the next."[47] Many of the educators I know report a rise of children with serious behavioral problems, with disrespectful demeanor and cruelty of words being at the top of the list. If we leave our children to their devices, if we don't put them in situations that teach empathy—face-to-face interaction, eye contact with other human beings—it's not surprising that they have trouble seeing the effects of their words on others. It's not surprising that they become cruel. We pay a high price when we bury our faces in our phones.

Secondly, and related to my first suggestion, we need to commit to the work of *building embodied friendships*. Many people turn to social media with the hope of finding deep relationships, but this is akin to running to the nearest gas station with the hope of picking up a fine wine. Or rummaging through your popcorn bucket with the hope of finding a perfectly cooked porterhouse. You're looking in the wrong place. A person might have ten thousand followers on social media but not one true friend. A person might have ten thousand followers and not *be* a true friend. The social internet brings shallow connection rather than deep community. Shallow connection is easier because it doesn't ask much of us. Why sit down, close my eyes, and focus my attention on a prayer for someone when I can just send her a prayer emoji? Why take a day off work to help someone move into his new house when I can just like a picture of his new house? Clicks of affirmation are not acts of loving sacrifice. Technology offers "the illusion of companionship without the demands of friendship."[48] As Koji

---

46. Turkle, *Reclaiming Conversation*, 3.
47. Turkle, *Reclaiming Conversation*, 170, citing Daniel Siegel.
48. Turkle, *Reclaiming Conversation*, 7.

says to John Wick, "Friendship means little when it's convenient."[49] Embodied friendships don't hide behind edits and filters. There's a realness to them. They don't play out in controllable environments or manageable amounts, one block of text at a time. There's a messiness to them. They take much more determination and patience to develop. There's a slowness to them. But this makes them slower to die.

Finally, we need to do the hard but good work of *staying put, not just in the real world, but in a particular place.* The internet brings the world to us in ways our great-grandparents never could have imagined. There's a positive side to this, of course. But one of the negative consequences is that we have been stripped of our locality: We have less local affection. One of the things I love about Wendell Berry's fiction is how deeply planted his characters are in their community of Port William. "Membership" in Berry's works refers both to people and a place ("the Port William Membership"). In his book *Hannah Coulter*, for example, the title character explains, "Members of Port William aren't trying to 'get someplace.' They think they *are* someplace."[50] Hannah continues, "Most people now are looking for 'a better place,' which means that a lot of them will end up in a worse one. . . . There is no 'better place' than this, not in *this* world. And it is by the place we've got, and our love for it and our keeping of it, that this world is joined to Heaven."[51]

Unlike Berry's characters, we're always trying to get somewhere else. And why wouldn't we? With the internet, we can "go" anywhere in a matter of seconds. I can watch a video of a YouTuber in London, then check social media to see what's new on the south island of New Zealand, hop over to a workout programmed by an athlete in Canada, and finally land on the latest headlines in the US. This leaves me feeling "over-stimulated but under-activated."[52] As McCracken says, "We can easily come to the point where we

49. Stahelski, *John Wick: Chapter 4*.
50. Berry, *Hannah Coulter*, 67.
51. Berry, *Hannah Coulter*, 83.
52. McCracken, *Wisdom Pyramid*, 31.

spend hours attending to headlines about things that will never affect us, debates about things we know little or nothing about, and problems we cannot solve. Meanwhile, as we are consumed by the 'far away' dramas of our social media spaces, we neglect the tangible realities of our immediate place."[53] Everyone wants to change the world, but nobody's willing to do the dishes. Everyone wants to remedy global poverty, but nobody sees the beggar at his own gate. How could we see him? Our faces are still stuck in our feeds, where the world's chaos comes rushing at our minds like a meteor, shattering our attention and sending it in a thousand different directions.

It's time to wake up to the people and the needs that are right here, where Sovereignty has stationed us. Stop trying to get somewhere else, somewhere better. Be *here*. As Berry says, "You can't act locally by thinking globally."[54] But if we all act locally, then in time the world—the *real* world—will become a different place.

---

53. McCracken, *Wisdom Pyramid*, 32.
54. Berry, "Out of Your Car, Off Your Horse," 23.

## 5

# Avarice

## All Is Advertisement

### COLLYER MANSION

COLLYER MANSION: IT'S "THE stuff of legend and the legend of stuff."[1]

Homer and Langley Collyer were brothers. They lived in Harlem in the first half of the twentieth century. The Collyers were born into a distinguished family. Both boys went to Columbia University: Homer received a degree in law, while Langley studied engineering and chemistry. In 1933, Homer lost his eyesight due to hemorrhages in the back of his eyes, so Langley quit his job to care for his brother, and both began to withdraw from society. As time passed, the brothers became fearful due to changes in the neighborhood. The largely upper-class area changed dramatically during the Great Depression. Talk of the Collyers' unconventional lifestyle spread throughout Harlem, and crowds began to gather outside their home. The unwelcomed attention only increased their fear—and their eccentricities.

After losing his eyesight, Homer didn't leave the home. Langley, on the other hand, would venture out after midnight in search of food and an assortment of other items. In 1938, *The New York*

---

1. Herring, *Hoarders*, 19.

## Deathly (De)Vices

*Times* published a story about the Collyer brothers, suggesting that they were hoarders who were sitting on piles of cash. Rumors like this led to several break-ins, but the burglars were never able to find the money, because once inside the house they discovered mountains of stuff to sort through. As an added security measure, Langley used his engineering skills to construct booby traps and tunnels among the vast collection of goods (and junk) that filled the house.

In 1947, an anonymous caller alerted the police that someone in the Collyers' home had died. The caller claimed that the stench of decomposition was emanating from the house. After a day's search, the police found the body of Homer, sitting bent over, with his head on his knees. But where was Langley? It took workers eighteen days to find him. In the end, workers removed over one hundred tons of stuff from Collyer Mansion: toys, bicycles, bowling balls, a collection of guns, chandeliers, tapestries, thousands of books, fourteen pianos, two organs (the instrument kind), pickled organs (the human kind), the chassis of a Model T, the folding top of a horse-drawn carriage, and the list goes on. The rooms in the house were packed almost to the ceilings, and this great mass of possessions was pierced by the tunnels Langley had dug. It was in one of those tunnels that his body finally was discovered. Police theorized that Langley was crawling through the tunnel to bring food to Homer when he accidentally tripped one of his own booby traps, entombing himself. Eighteen days they searched for Langley. Finally, they found him: buried beneath his belongings, suffocated by his stuff.[2]

### THE DESIRE TO ACQUIRE

When it comes to our possessions, there are only two possible outcomes: they rot, or we do. Avarice is blind to this truth. Simply stated, avarice is the desire to acquire more and more. The

---

2. For an analysis of the Collyers, see Herring, *Hoarders*, 19–50. The basic details recounted here come from Herring's work and *Harlem World*, "Legendary Collyer Brothers Harlem NY 1881–1947."

avaricious person chases creature comforts, thinking they will satisfy his deepest desires. She is consumed by the quest for wealth, possessed by the thought of more possessions. Countless characters from film and literature have embodied this capital vice. In the original *Pirates of the Caribbean,* far and away the best film in the series, Captain Barbossa's story of the Aztec gold captures the final result of avarice with haunting precision. (As you read, be sure to imagine Geoffrey Rush's creepy pirate voice.)

> Find it, we did. There be the chest. Inside be the gold. And we took 'em all! We spent 'em, and traded 'em. And frittered 'em away on drink and food and pleasurable company. The more we gave 'em away, the more we came to realize . . . the drink would not satisfy. Food turned to ash in our mouths. And all the pleasurable company in the world could not slake our lust. We are cursed men . . . . Compelled by greed we were, but now we are consumed by it.[3]

None so memorably portray avarice as the villain of Charles Dickens's ghost story of Christmas, Ebenezer Scrooge. Dickens describes Scrooge as "a tight-fisted hand at the grindstone . . . a squeezing, wrenching, grasping, scraping, clutching, covetous, old sinner!"[4] Avarice is a condition of the heart that shows itself in the hands. Scrooge was "tight-fisted . . . squeezing . . . grasping." A person can be wealthy without being greedy. It's the *grip* that makes the difference.

Among other things, J. R. R. Tolkien's classic *The Hobbit* is a tale of avarice, or to use the term Tolkien himself coined, dragon-sickness.[5] During the final battle, Thorin Oakenshield, leader of the dwarves, is mortally wounded. His friend Bilbo kneels beside him to say goodbye: "Farewell, King under the Mountain! This is a

---

3. Verbinski, *Pirates of the Caribbean: The Curse of the Black Pearl.*

4. Dickens, *Christmas Carol,* 2.

5. Tolkien, *Hobbit,* 23: "Dragons steal gold and jewels, you know, from men and elves and dwarves, wherever they can find them; and they guard their plunder as long as they live (which is practically for ever, unless they are killed)."

## Deathly (De)Vices

bitter adventure, if it must end so; and not a mountain of gold can amend it. Yet I am glad that I have shared in your perils—that has been more than any Baggins deserves." With his last breath, Thorin replies, "If more of us valued food and cheer and song above hoarded gold, it would be a merrier world. But sad or merry, I must leave it now. Farewell!"[6] With respect to money and material possessions, all humans, Hobbits, and dwarves will depart as they came: empty-handed. This truth should have a profound effect on the way we think about possessions *now*.

Consider the words of 1 Tim 6:6–10:

> But godliness with contentment is great gain, for we brought nothing into the world, and we cannot take anything out of the world. But if we have food and clothing, with these we will be content. But those who desire to be rich fall into temptation, into a snare, into many senseless and harmful desires that plunge people into ruin and destruction. For the love of money is a root of all kinds of evils. It is through this craving that some have wandered away from the faith and pierced themselves with many pangs.

When we entered this world, we brought nothing with us; and when we exit this world, our carry-on items will be the same. In the words of Job, "Naked I came from my mother's womb, and naked shall I return" (Job 1:21). Mindful of the impermanence of our possessions, we should be content with life's necessities: a roof over our heads, bread on the table, and shoes on our feet. The writer of 1 Timothy doesn't indicate that to have *more* than life's necessities is sinful. Later in the letter, he'll urge the rich in the community to remember that God is the source of their riches; thus, they should be ready to use these riches for God's purposes (1 Tim 6:17–19). Again, a person can be wealthy without being greedy. The issue here in 1 Tim 6:6–10 is *desire*: not being driven by the desire to acquire more and more.[7] Money itself is not the problem, but "the

---

6. Tolkien, *Hobbit*, 262–63.

7. Johnson, *First and Second Letters to Timothy*, 294, says that the author emphasizes "the willingness to be satisfied with what one has, rather than having that craving disease that always seeks more."

## AVARICE

love of money" (v. 10). Through this craving called avarice "some have wandered away from the faith," that is, they've chosen money as their master.[8] And in pursuing their dream of more wealth, actually they create their own nightmare, piercing themselves with many pangs (v. 10). "A life driven by such constant craving is a form of self-torture."[9]

Returning to the idea of dragon-sickness, Tolkien's friend and fellow Inkling C. S. Lewis illustrates the grotesque and self-enslaving nature of avarice in his poem "The Dragon Speaks."[10] As Lewis's dragon reflects on his life, he recalls how he wooed his wife, whom eventually he ate. In his later years, the dragon regrets doing so, though for a selfish reason: "Gold would have been the safer." Two beasts are better than one for guarding the hoard. Now, for fear that man at any moment might come to steal his treasure, the old, lugubrious dragon remains in his cave-prison, leaving but once in winter and twice in summer to drink from the rock pool. "Oh, Lord, that made the dragon," he prays, "grant me Thy peace! But ask not that I should give up the gold, nor move, nor die; others would get the gold. Kill, rather, Lord, the men and the other dragons that I may sleep, go when I will to drink." The beast's avarice has taken everything from him, even his freedom. It's an unforgettable example of the point made in the 1 Timothy text: A life motivated by the love of money is a form of self-torment. The self-inflicted pain stops only when life ends, when with empty hands the avaricious beast passes from this world.

---

8. See Matt 6:24; Luke 16:13. Lewis, *Mere Christianity*, 213–14, writes, "One of the dangers of having a lot of money is that you may be quite satisfied with the kinds of happiness money can give and so fail to realise your need for God. If everything seems to come simply by signing cheques, you may forget that you are at every moment totally dependent on God."

9. Johnson, *First and Second Letters to Timothy*, 296. Towner, *Letters to Timothy and Titus*, 405, writes of the self-torture: "Any number of things might be included, from the personal emotional torments of unfulfilled dreams (of wealth) and damaged reputations to the relationships destroyed when desire for wealth overrules brotherly love."

10. King, *Collected Poems of C. S. Lewis*, 232–33.

## Deathly (De)Vices

In Luke 12, two brothers are arguing over the family inheritance. One of the brothers comes to Jesus, asking him to arbitrate. Instead, Jesus says, "One's life does not consist in the abundance of his possessions" (v. 15). Then he tells a short, sharp story to make his point come to life. Once upon a time, there was a rich man, a farmer whose land produced plentifully. Did you catch that? It's subtle, but important. As Jesus tells the story, he says *the land* produced plentifully (v. 16); he doesn't say *the farmer* produced plentifully. Jesus gives ultimate credit for the good year not to the farmer, but to God, the Creator of the land, the Sustainer of all life. But the farmer can't see this. This farmer has had such a good year that he has insufficient storage for his harvest. In his avarice, he devises a plan—one he thinks will ensure a long and happy life. He decides to tear down his current barns. A savvy solution, indeed. Rather than building additional barns and thus taking up land that might otherwise be used for farming, he demolishes the current storage facility and designs a new one, a bigger one. Once his construction project is complete, the farmer anticipates a life of luxury and security: "I will say to my soul, 'Soul, you have ample goods laid up for many years; relax, eat, drink, be merry'" (v. 19).

The farmer could have shared with his neighbors. He could have seen in this surplus the hand of God entrusting him with the ministry of generosity. Instead, he thinks only of himself and does what he believes will secure his comfort, both now and in the future. But he's wrong. The parable in Luke 12 emphasizes how very little control this man has over his life, despite what he thinks. "Even what he thinks is most intimately his own—his soul—is only on loan and can be demanded at any time."[11] In the final scene of the parable, God comes to the farm. Of all the NT parables, this is the only one in which God himself appears as an actor in the narrative.[12] One day, with no notice at all, God interrupts the farmer's moneymaking and merrymaking, calls him a fool, requires his soul, and asks, "All these things you have prepared, whose will they be?" (v. 20). The question lingers. And the rich man disappears.

---

11. Snodgrass, *Stories with Intent*, 399.
12. Snodgrass, *Stories with Intent*, 394.

With respect to our possessions, there are only two possible outcomes: they rot, or we do. Consistently, the Bible warns us about being driven by the desire to acquire more and more. But this is not the only message we hear, and probably it's not the loudest. Today, everywhere we turn, we're told that to find true happiness—the good life—we need more money, more stuff. And our devices play a dominant role in this deception.

## ADVERTISING IN A POST-AD WORLD

To understand how our devices awaken avarice in our hearts, we need to think about the people on the other side of the devices. "What do you want to be when you grow up?" The question has been asked of children for ages, and it has a new most common answer: "I want to be a YouTuber." A 2018 study of children ages eight to twelve found that 30 percent of kids in the United Kingdom and 29 percent of kids in the United States aspire to be a vlogger or YouTuber: the most common answer, followed by teacher, athlete, musician, and astronaut. A similar study conducted in 2019 found that 54 percent of teenagers and adults under age forty would be a digital influencer if given the opportunity.[13] Why do so many children, teenagers, and young adults aspire to be an influencer? Because the influencer lifestyle presents the possibility that we could get paid to share pictures and videos of ourselves, doing the things we like to do. It's a way to satisfy our vainglory *and* to make some big money. The world will see us, people will want to be like us, and we'll get paid in the process. No wonder the influencer lifestyle has greater appeal than the teacher lifestyle.[14]

The influencer is decidedly a twenty-first-century occupation. By going back to the inception, we'll get a better grasp of how influencers work today—and how they work on us. Emily Hund is a research affiliate at the Center on Digital Culture and Society at the University of Pennsylvania. In her book *The Influencer*

---

13. Martin, *Wolf in Their Pockets*, 45.

14. Though the influencer lifestyle isn't all it's cracked up to be. See Mills, "YouTube Gave Me Everything. Then I Grew Up."

*Industry*, Hund offers a critical history of the influencer industry's formative years in the US, tracking its development "from a haphazard group of creative people scrambling for work in the face of the Great Recession to today's multi-faceted, multibillion-dollar industry with expanding global impact."[15] Hund argues that as the first decade of the twenty-first century ended, a perfect storm of technological, economic, cultural, and industrial factors gave rise to the influencer industry.[16]

First, the technological factors: The advent of software like Blogger and WordPress made it easy, even for non–tech-savvy people, to publish material online. Social media sites such as Twitter, Facebook, and YouTube emerged, making the process of sharing information and connecting with people online easier than ever. Social media spread like wildfire. In 2005, only 5 percent of American adults used a social networking platform. Ten years later, nearly 70 percent did.[17] Technologically enabled entrepreneurship also became popular, as sites like eBay and Etsy enabled global commerce.

Second, the cultural factors: These technological changes gave people direct lines to "publics" they never had before and harmonized with the cultural valorization of entrepreneurship, the increasingly individualized nature of work that had begun to take hold in the 1990s. As institutional distrust festered, the millennial generation had new options for independent work.

Third, the economic factors: As millions of people lost their jobs in the wake of the 2008 global financial crisis, many under- or unemployed individuals—especially aspiring creative professionals—turned to the internet and its burgeoning social media platforms to network, build their reputations, and attract employers.

Finally, the industrial factors: The economic crisis expedited media industry shifts that had been approaching since the launch of the commercial web. Journalism was becoming a less viable career path as job opportunities dried up. Advertisers were

15. Hund, *Influencer Industry*, 6.
16. The following discussion is based on Hund, *Influencer Industry*, 12–35.
17. Hund, *Influencer Industry*, 24.

searching for more effective outlets than the print establishment. In the digital influencer, advertisers found a new hope. Thanks to their personality-driven content, influencers offered advertisers audiences that were conveniently segmented. Hund explains, "For a clothing brand looking to advertise their size-inclusive line, the loyal audience of a woman in her late twenties who creates focused blog and Instagram content on the topic offers a clearer targeted opportunity than the print pages of *Glamour* to reach that niche."[18] By 2010, retail brands understood that these digital content creators offered direct lines to the buying public.[19]

In ensuing years, the influencers, marketers, brands, and technologists involved in the influencer industry created a whole new ecosystem in which people encounter information and products. Influencers offer seamless integration of content with the ability to shop. In what many experts refer to as a "post-ad world," where consumers avoid blatant advertising, influencers provide companies a crucial means of getting the pitch to the public. Hund writes, "While many influencers identify themselves as being 'fueled by passion' and their work being a 'creative outlet,' collectively, they are marketing juggernauts and vital components of the retail system."[20]

From the influencer's side of the device, you and I are economic assets. The influencer industry is a system that monetizes relationships. Followers equal dollars. According to the influencer management platform Traackr, 72 percent of major brands dedicate a sizable portion of their marketing budgets to influencers.[21] Joe Gagliese, one of the co-founders of Viral Nation, an influencer

18. Hund, *Influencer Industry*, 26.

19. Stokel-Walker, *YouTubers*, 15, writes, "YouTube is different to a conventional media company: its reach is wider, its diversity broader, its demographic younger, and its power stronger. All that has caught the attention of big business."

20. Hund, *Influencer Industry*, 29.

21. Lieber, "How and Why Do Influencers Make So Much Money?" Burton, *Self-Made*, 222, reports a slightly higher number: as of 2021, influencing had become a $13.8 billion industry with 75 percent of American brands budgeting for influencers.

## Deathly (De)Vices

agency that boasts the ability to "create the most viral, captivating and ROI-focused social media influencer campaigns for global brands" reports that a micro-influencer, someone with 10,000 to 50,000 followers, earns a minimum of a few thousand dollars per post.[22] Influencers with up to 1 million followers can get $10,000 per post, depending on the platform. Those with 1 million followers and up might make $100,000 on a single post.[23] Why such an astronomical amount for a single social media post? Because the brand knows that the influencer's "relationship" with the followers means he or she holds sway over their purchasing habits.[24]

The industry values the *idea* of authenticity. This is what enables the seamless integration of content and shopping. For example, my sons love to watch the videos of a YouTuber named Bricksie, a self-proclaimed AFOL: adult fan of LEGO. Every day, Bricksie shoots a video from his headquarters, where's he's built an epic LEGO world. In each video, he creates a new masterpiece to add to his world. Bricksie, whose real name is Jordan, is an affable guy. He has a family. He seems like the type of guy you could bump into at the hardware store. If you're into LEGO, his videos are entertaining. And he's not trying to sell you LEGO products, he's just building LEGO products—again and again. No commercial breaks. Just LEGO construction. And you know what both my sons are saving their money for right now? LEGO products. There are no commercials because *Bricksie is the commercial*. The brand's message is intertwined with the influencer's own message; in a sense, the two have become one. Who knows where Bricksie ends and LEGO begins?[25]

---

22. Stokel-Walker, *YouTubers*, 90, divides influencers into four categories: nano, micro, macro, and elite.

23. Lieber, "How and Why Do Influencers Make So Much Money?"

24. Stokel-Walker, *YouTubers*, 89, speaks of "the hypnotic pull" YouTubers have over their viewers. Burton, *Self-Made*, 224, writes, "When it comes to how we spend our money, we trust influencers."

25. Smith, *Internet Is Not What You Think It Is*, 20, quips, "Under these circumstances, one wants to say: 'I do not even understand *of myself* what is advertisement and what is not advertisement'" (emphasis original).

## AVARICE

For those of us on the viewer side of the device, the sales pitch never stops. This is one of the unique features of our day. Advertising has been around since the dawn of civilization. But with mediums like newspaper and magazine, it's easy to opt out: skip a section or page. When I was growing up, watching television shows like *Saved by the Bell*, *Home Improvement*, and *Friends*, the commercial break was when you ran to the kitchen for a snack, or started a fight with your brother—anything *but* watch the commercials. Justin Smith, professor of history and philosophy of science at the University of Paris, captures the present technocultural moment: "Today, all is advertisement. Or, to put this somewhat more cautiously, there is no part of our most important technology products and services that is kept cordoned off as a safe space from the commercial interests of the companies that own them."[26]

Another unique feature of our day is the bidirectional nature of advertising. When my grandfather came to the advertisements, he could simply stop reading his newspaper, and he never had to worry about *the newspaper reading him*. "The new advertisement landscape by contrast is one that functions bidirectionally, monitoring potential customers' behavior, attentional habits, and inclinations, and developing numerous technological prods and traps that together make it nearly impossible to decide to exit this commercial nexus."[27] According to Smith, one term that has begun circulating in social media to describe someone who spends time online is "data cow." Vivid. Unsettling. Users are like domesticated animals, not giving our fluids, but "giving something that has proven more valuable to the new economy than milk ever was in the system of industrial agriculture: information about who we are, what we do, what we think, what we fear."[28] Today, all is advertisement. And the advertisement is studying us, building our

---

26. Smith, *Internet Is Not What You Think It Is*, 18.

27. Smith, *Internet Is Not What You Think It Is*, 19. See also Hari, *Stolen Focus*, 124–42.

28. Smith, *Internet Is Not What You Think It Is*, 15. Similarly, Vaidhyanathan, *Antisocial Media*, 203, writes, "We have become data-producing farm animals, domesticated and dependent. We are the cows. Facebook clicks on us."

epic digital biographies, learning what baits work best on us, what times of day we're most likely to bite.

If it's "nearly impossible to decide to exit this commercial nexus," as Smith suggests, then the best approach is to limit our use of technology in the first place, and the social internet in particular. In Jaron Lanier's judgment, deleting social media is the only way to remain autonomous "in a world where you are under constant surveillance and are constantly prodded by algorithms run by some of the richest corporations in history, which have no way of making money except by being paid to manipulate your behavior."[29] We need the discipline modeled by Wendell Berry in his essay "The Joy of Sales Resistance." Commenting on certain technology of the 1990s, he writes: "My joy comes from my instantaneous knowledge that I am not going to buy [these technological inventions]. When the inevitable saleswoman comes to tell me that I cannot be up-to-date, or intelligent, or creative, or handsome, or young, or eligible for the sexual favors of so fair a creature as herself unless I buy these products, dear reader, I am not going to do it."[30] In our day, the pull toward avarice is complex, many-tentacled, involving various platforms and online personalities. Some of us may need to abstain from certain technological inventions like social media. At a minimum, we need to curb our time on our devices and, when online, do our best to remain alert to the commercial nexus. For most of us, *media consciousness* is the way forward. As Neil Postman put it nearly forty years ago, "No medium is excessively dangerous if its users understand what its dangers are."[31] Just remember that when you're watching Bricksie, he's selling you LEGOs, even as he's not selling you LEGOs.

---

29. Lanier, *Ten Arguments for Deleting Your Social Media Accounts Right Now*, 2. See also Harber, "Social Media Is a Spiritual Distortion Zone"; Hari, *Stolen Focus*, 127, who speaks of "surveillance capitalism." Surprisingly, given Smith's strong critique of the internet as a universal surveillance device, he does not suggest deletion of social media as a way forward. See Smith, *Internet Is Not What You Think It Is*, 51.

30. Berry, "Joy of Sales Resistance," xx–xxi.

31. Postman, *Amusing Ourselves to Death*, 161.

*AVARICE*

## THE PARADOX OF GENEROSITY

A predominant message of our technocultural moment is that we'll be happier when we've acquired *more* than what we have now. On the contrary, Scripture teaches us that we'll be happier with *less* than what we have now. In Acts 20, the great missionary, Paul, gathers the church leaders of Ephesus for final instructions before he travels elsewhere. Among these final instructions is an important word about generosity: what some have called "the paradox of generosity." "Remember the words of the Lord Jesus, how he himself said, 'It is more blessed to give than to receive'" (Acts 20:35).[32] Well-being, abiding joy, purposeful living: these things come to us as we give to others. We will be *more* satisfied with *less* than what we have. This is not only a religious teaching; it's also a sociological fact.

In their book, *The Paradox of Generosity: Giving We Receive, Grasping We Lose*, Christian Smith and Hilary Davidson contend, "Generosity is paradoxical. Those who give, receive back in turn. By spending ourselves for others' well-being, we enhance our own standing. In letting go of some of what we own, we better secure our own lives. By giving ourselves away, we ourselves move toward flourishing."[33] In the years leading up to the publication of their book, Smith and Davidson participated in a study called the "Science of Generosity Initiative" at the University of Notre Dame. Their empirical social-science research confirms precisely what the NT teaches: The more generous people are, the more happiness, health, and purpose in life they enjoy. "People rightly say that money cannot buy happiness. But money and happiness are still related in a curious way. Happiness can be the result, not of spending more money on oneself, but rather of giving money away to others. Generous financial givers are happier people."[34]

32. Interestingly, we don't know when Jesus said this. The specific saying is not found in the Gospels. But the essence of the saying is found in Luke 6:35-36, 38.

33. Smith and Davidson, *Paradox of Generosity*, 1.

34. Smith and Davidson, *Paradox of Generosity*, 11-12. They note, however, that for generosity to enhance a person's well-being, "generosity cannot

## Deathly (De)Vices

Like a child in a Chinese finger trap, our gut reaction concerning our money and possessions is to pull as hard as possible, but this only tightens the trap, better securing the prisoner. Only by freely letting go of our resources, by pushing them in a counterintuitive and countercultural direction, will we escape the trap. Rather than living to acquire, to accumulate, to grasp and spend for ourselves, we need instead to live *into* the paradox of generosity. By truly desiring the good of others, and by developing generous habits, we will find ourselves happier, healthier, more purposeful in life, and, wonder of wonders, *more Godlike*. For us, God the Father spared no expense, giving his own Son over to the power of death so that through faith in him we might have forgiveness of sin and newness of life. In the action of giving, we become like the God who gives; we display *his* generosity to the world.

---

be faked in order to achieve some other, more valued, self-serving end. Generosity *itself* needs to be desired" (7, emphasis original). Contrast with the influencer MrBeast, who has built a YouTube empire on quasi philanthropy, the sort of calculated generosity that turns charity into content. See Read, "How MrBeast Became the Willy Wonka of YouTube."

# 6

# Wrath

Tension Gets Attention

### ADAPTIVE CRUISE CONTROL

WE NAME OUR CARS. For the longest time, we were a one-car family. But as our sons' activities and our responsibilities increased, eventually we bit the bullet and bought a second vehicle. I drive a blue Chevy Colorado named Stormbreaker. My wife drives a bright red Chevy Blazer named Wanda (Maximoff). Wanda is the more sophisticated of the two—like my wife. Unbeknownst to me when I bought her (the car, not my wife), she has a feature called adaptive cruise control. Perhaps you've used this feature in your vehicles for years, but I discovered it only recently, and when I did, I was like a kid on Christmas morning. It revolutionized my interstate driving. Adaptive cruise control uses sensory technology—cameras, lasers, and radar equipment—to create an idea of how close one car is to another. I set my cruise at seventy-seven—I mean, seventy—and off to Orlando I go. In the old days, if I approached a driver traveling at a lesser speed, he would force me to hit the brake, break my cruise control setting, and begin driving manually again. Oh, the frustration! But now, equipped with adaptive cruise control, Wanda senses when the vehicle in front of me is traveling at a lesser speed, and she drops her speed accordingly, maintaining a safe distance between me and the driver ahead. When that driver increases his speed or changes lanes, Wanda senses it and automatically returns to the speed I set. As a driver, I simply keep my eyes on the road, and Wanda manages my speed.

While on my way to Gainesville one day, basking in the glory of this driver-assistance technology, it occurred to me that the internet does something similar, though with the opposite effect. Rather than *slowing* our emotions and communication, it *quickens* them. Rather than making us more *cautious* and *courteous*, it makes us more *indignant* and *aggressive*. As a user, I simply keep my eyes on my feed, and the web manages my speed, moving me away from slow and careful reflection to quick, heated reaction. A person who turns to the social internet with the hope of finding deep relationships is searching for the right thing in the wrong place. Equally foolish is the errand of turning to the social internet with the hope of finding mostly sensible and charitable expression of thought. "If the romantic vision of the internet is a massive Areopagus, where the common people gather to penetrate mysteries and exchange ideas, the reality of the web is more like a gladiator arena."[1]

## ANGRY JESUS

Of the seven *ways of being* we've been studying, wrath is the trickiest, because it's the only of the seven that is found in God himself. The Bible speaks of God's *glory*, but not his *vainglory*. It never speaks of God's *avarice* or God's *lust*—of course not. But it does at times speak of God's *wrath*, his *anger*. And yet, the Bible teaches us that God is holy, perfectly pure, utterly sinless—*vice*less. The apostle John writes, "God is light, and in him is no darkness at all" (1 John 1:5). If God experiences anger, and God is without sin, then anger is not always sinful. Sometimes, wrath is an inappropriate disposition; at other times, it's an appropriate one. That's why this is the trickiest of the seven.

---

1. James, *Digital Liturgies*, 92.

## Wrath

An assessment of our own anger should begin with an understanding of Jesus, *angry* Jesus. In John 11, Jesus receives word that his good friend, Lazarus, is sick. Lazarus's sisters send word to Jesus regarding their brother's illness, for they know of Jesus' healing power, and they expect him to intervene immediately. In a counterintuitive move, Jesus intentionally delays his journey to see this beloved Bethany family. Two days later, by means of supernatural insight, Jesus announces to his disciples that Lazarus is dead. Already in the narrative, he demonstrates that he has some special power with respect to death: from afar, he knows precisely when the grave has claimed his friend. Once Lazarus has taken his final breath, Jesus says to his disciples, "*Our* friend Lazarus has fallen asleep, but *I* go to awaken him" (v. 11).

The two-day delay combined with a two-day journey to Bethany means that Jesus arrives on the fourth day, ensuring that no one can interpret his actions as a mere resuscitation. Ancient sources attest the belief that the soul hovered over the body of a deceased person for a period of three days, intending to re-enter it. But, as soon as decomposition set in, the soul would depart, making death irreversible.[2] According to the Jewish funeral custom, the family would have hired professional mourners, people to play instruments and women to weep and wail for the dead.[3] Jesus arrives at this house of death to make an unforgettable statement, in essence to say, "Death, I've got your address. I know where you live. And I'm coming for you."

The sisters of the deceased fall at Jesus' feet, weeping uncontrollably. Then, John describes Jesus' disposition: "He was deeply moved in his spirit and greatly troubled" (v. 33). English translations routinely soften the language here. In extrabiblical Greek, the crucial word *embrimaomai* can refer to the snorting of horses. When applied to humans, invariably the term suggests anger.[4] "In his spirit" is equivalent to "in himself." Thus, Jesus' inward reaction is *outrage*. The object of Jesus' anger has been identified as death

---

2. Carson, *Gospel According to John*, 411.
3. Köstenberger, *John*, 338.
4. Carson, *Gospel According to John*, 415.

itself or as the realm of Satan represented by death.[5] The same sin and death that stirred his anger also generates his grief: "Jesus wept" (v. 35).[6] This compressed verse is the climactic instance in John's Gospel of Jesus' humanity.[7] Tears are liquid love. To shed them here is to show his love for life, not just Lazarus's, but all life. Anger stirred, tears flowing, Jesus speaks. First, he speaks to his Father in prayer. Then, he speaks to his friend in the tomb: "Lazarus, come out!" (v. 43). His emotions evolve into actions, though actions with a particular purpose. *Angry* Jesus speaks words of *life*.

## ANGRY LIKE JESUS

Jesus is not moved to anger often, but when he is, his anger never is self-serving.[8] He's angry when Lazarus lies in the tomb; he's not angry when he hangs on the cross (Luke 23:34). Jesus models what he teaches his disciples: "If anyone slaps you on the right cheek, turn to him the other also. And if anyone would sue you and take your tunic, let him have your cloak as well" (Matt 5:39–40). Jesus is not concerned with the protection of his own reputation or property. Threaten these, and righteous anger doesn't burn. The key question for each of us to consider is "What is my anger guarding?" Anger always seeks to protect something it loves. At its core, anger is very simple. It says, "I'm against *that* because *that* is against something I care about."[9] Figure out what love lies at the source of your displeasure, and you will have taken the first step toward determining if yours is a Jesus-like anger. The next thing we need to think about is how to express the anger we're feeling.

---

5. See the discussion in Köstenberger, *John*, 340.

6. Carson, *Gospel According to John*, 416, writes, "Those who follow Jesus as his disciples today do well to learn the same tension—that grief and compassion without outrage reduce to mere sentiment, while outrage without grief hardens into self-righteous arrogance and irascibility."

7. Köstenberger, *John*, 341.

8. DeYoung, *Glittering Vices*, 140.

9. Powlison, *Good and Angry*, 39.

Scripture sets the parameters for our active displeasure. Of the scriptural writers, James and Paul are particularly helpful. First, James tells us, "Know this, my beloved brothers: let every person be quick to hear, slow to speak, slow to anger; for the anger of man does not produce the righteousness of God" (Jas 1:19–20). James writes of a swiftness of the ears and a slowness of the tongue and temper. The admonition to display wisdom by listening much and speaking little is common in Proverbs (e.g., 10:19; 11:12; 13:3; 17:28; 29:11). Uncontrolled anger leads to an unbridled tongue and an unbridled tongue to a world of unrighteousness (Jas 3:6). When our anger is non-Jesus-like, we do not "produce the righteousness of God," James says, that is, we do not cultivate those right relationships God desires for his creatures; rather, we scorch our communities (Jas 3:5).[10] James's warning amounts to this: Many (and perhaps most) occurrences should *not* stir our anger to the point of human-to-human expression. When someone cuts me off in traffic, when the referee makes a bad call in the game, or when the line at the store is Disney World long, I shouldn't respond with outrage, but with grace and gentleness. Gentleness isn't the absence of anger. In that moment when the guy cuts me off in traffic, I *feel* anger bubbling up within me. Gentleness is the Spirit-empowered management of my anger in such a way that I don't vocalize it to the offender.[11] Instead, I vocalize it to God in prayer.[12] The Psalms, and especially the imprecatory psalms (i.e., psalms of anger), give us permission to bring even our fiercest feelings to God, to pour them out in prayer, and to process them in his presence. In prayer, the heart is unburdened of its animosity by the committal of the entire matter to God.[13]

Whereas James urges a general slowness to vocalize anger to our offenders, Paul provides instructions for that smaller number

---

10. Johnson, *Letter of James*, 200.

11. DeYoung, *Glittering Vices*, 161, writes, "Those with the virtue of gentleness have mastered their anger, rather than being mastered by it."

12. Rightly, Willimon, *Sinning Like a Christian*, 66, says that anger should be expressed "in church, in prayer, in conversation with God."

13. Bruce, *Epistles to the Colossians, to Philemon, and to the Ephesians*, 361.

of occasions that do require loving confrontation. In Eph 4:26–27, he writes, "Be angry and do not sin; do not let the sun go down on your anger, and give no opportunity to the devil." Paul *permits* and then immediately *restricts* anger. As the NIV translates it, "In your anger do not sin." The anger itself may be justifiable, but where anger is present "a potentially sinful situation exists."[14] Mindful of this, those who are angry should take practical steps to avoid sin. This includes dealing with anger swiftly. Probably, we shouldn't interpret Paul's "don't-let-the-sun-go-down" statement literally. It's not the case that if you happen to be in Alaska in the summertime then you have much longer to be angry with someone. Paul's intention is to warn us about the danger of allowing anger to fester and grow into a non-Jesus-like expression. Typical of Ephesians, Paul explains the result in terms of spiritual warfare. When we harbor anger, we give an "opportunity to the devil." We lower the drawbridge, allowing the enemy to invade the castle. The devil's lackeys love perpetually angry people, knowing that unresolved anger is their way into the Christian community, their golden opportunity to divide God's people and distract us from the mission. For the kingdom's sake, then, cases of anger serious enough to warrant loving confrontation should be addressed swiftly (Eph 4:26–27), privately (Matt 18:15), and as calmly and thoughtfully as possible.[15] "Rash words are like sword thrusts, but the tongue of the wise brings healing" (Prov 12:18). We don't want to wield our words impetuously, like a young knight out to save the world by thrusting his sword at everything that takes a step in the wrong direction. Rather, we want to wield our words carefully, like a seasoned surgeon whose every stroke of the scalpel brings healing.

14. Thielman, *Ephesians*, 313–4.

15. For guidance on when and how to initiate constructive conflict, see Powlison, *Good and Angry*, 88–103, 149–70; Reinke, *12 Ways Your Phone Is Changing You*, 163–75. We would do well to remember Bruce's admonition: "There is a subtle temptation to regard my anger as righteous indignation and other people's anger as sheer bad temper" (Bruce, *Epistles to the Colossians, to Philemon, and to the Ephesians*, 361).

Always, the goal of such engagement is forgiveness and restoration of the relationship (Eph 4:32).[16] Refusing to confront an offense biblically and to forgive our offender has the same self-torturous end that we observed when considering avarice. We think that refusing to forgive that person who wronged us will hurt them, when actually it hurts us. As Anne Lamott puts it, "Not forgiving is like drinking rat poison and then waiting for the rat to die."[17] Our English word *wrath* comes from the same Anglo-Saxon root as the word *wreath*. To be poisoned by wrath is to be twisted out of your normal shape. That same Anglo-Saxon root also gives us the word *wraith*, an old word for a ghost or spirit that can't find rest. According to legend, spirits stay in the place where something hideous occurred, unable to get over the hurt. If we don't deal with our wrath through forgiveness, we will become wraith-like, morphing into a restless soul, tormented by the past, forever a prisoner to it.[18]

## MORE ENRAGING = MORE ENGAGING

Scripture enjoins us to be slow to anger and quick to resolve anger by speaking words of life, praying and working toward reconciliation. The social internet spurs precisely the opposite behaviors: It wants us to be quick to anger and slow to resolve it. As Chris Martin says, "The problem for us is that the most prevalent communications medium in the world today promotes conflict more than any communications medium in human history, so to live at peace with all takes a measure of discipline that arguably no generation

---

16. It's helpful to differentiate *internal* or *attitudinal* forgiveness from *interpersonal* or *transacted* forgiveness. The former refers to forgiving another person before God and must always happen. The latter refers to the reconciliation of two parties, which is a goal to pursue, but not a certainty. As Powlison, *Good and Angry*, 86, says, "It takes two to reconcile, just like it takes two to make war. But one can forgive, even when the other is still at war. It is called loving your enemy."

17. Lamott, *Traveling Mercies*, 134.

18. Keller, *Forgive*, 163.

## Deathly (De)Vices

of Christians has had to muster."[19] In 2020, *The Wall Street Journal* published a piece titled "Facebook Executives Shut Down Efforts to Make the Site Less Divisive."[20] The article chronicles how Facebook commissioned an internal effort to better understand how its platform shaped user behavior and how the company might address potential harm. Having conducted their study, the team brought a blunt message to senior executives: "Our algorithms exploit the human brain's attraction to divisiveness." If left unchecked, Facebook would feed users "more and more divisive content in an effort to gain user attention and increase time on platform." Mark Zuckerberg and other senior executives shelved the basic research, blocked efforts to apply its conclusions to Facebook products, and continued their lucrative labor of aggravating anger.

The key finding cited above is worth considering more deeply: "Our algorithms exploit the human brain's attraction to divisiveness." "Algorithm" is shorthand for corporate AI, a somewhat mysterious machine-learning and -recommending system. Max Fisher, author of *The Chaos Machine*, confesses that no one quite knows how the algorithms that govern social media work. "The systems operate semi-autonomously, their methods beyond human grasp."[21] There's an incentive to remain ignorant, he adds. "Check how the goose gets those golden eggs and you might not like what you find. You might even have to give them back."[22] The system's all-seeing eye tracks everything we do online: what we watch, how long we watch it, and what we click on next. Monitoring millions of users, the system accrues the largest database on viewer preferences ever assembled, which it searches constantly for patterns. The best villains are the ones who know how to stay focused. Voldemort had one main goal: kill Harry Potter. Thanos

---

19. Martin, *Wolf in Their Pockets*, 112.

20. Horwitz and Seetharaman, "Facebook Executives Shut Down Efforts to Make the Site Less Divisive."

21. Fisher, *Chaos Machine*, 105.

22. Fisher, *Chaos Machine*, 105.

had one goal: wipe out half of all life. This invisible villain has a single focus: maximize humanity's time online.[23]

Imagine you've just received a new dog from a breeder.[24] The first morning you awake to find your new pet sitting at the foot of your bed, staring at you intently. Near the bed are three items the dog has fetched for you: a ball, a pair of socks, and a dead rodent. Horrified, you yell at the dog. But this dog isn't like other pets. It's immune to shame and deaf to scolding. It knows only how to watch you, keenly, observing what gets your attention. You bring your spouse into the room to see the dead rodent your new pet has fetched. It's so outrageous that you decide to take a few pictures so you can share the story with your friends. The dog sees it all, and then it scampers off. The next morning, it returns to the foot of your bed with three new objects: a creepy doll head, a deer skull, and a rotting log in the shape of a femur. Why such a morbid selection? Your curious canine watched how you reacted to the dead rodent, and it placed before you a similar, though more extreme, set of items.

Johann Hari highlights a quirk of human behavior, or what I prefer to call an expression of our fallen condition: "We will stare at something negative and outrageous for a lot longer than we will stare at something positive or calm."[25] We stare at the car crash longer than we stare at the farmer selling fresh strawberries on the side on the road. For the first time in human history, the majority of content we consume is controlled by algorithms, and designers are aware of our "negativity bias," so algorithms recommend the most enraging options. "If it's more enraging, it's more engaging."[26] According to Hari, to make your YouTube video most likely to be picked up by the algorithm, put one of the following words in the title: "hates," "obliterates," "slams," or "destroys." Tristan Harris, cofounder of the Center for Humane Technology, explains, "Outrage

---

23. Fisher, *Chaos Machine*, 108–9.

24. This illuminating analogy comes from Rose-Stockwell, *Outrage Machine*, 101.

25. Hari, *Stolen Focus*, 131.

26. Hari, *Stolen Focus*, 131.

just spreads faster than something that's not outrage. When you open the blue Facebook icon, you're activating the AI, which tries to figure out the perfect thing it can show you that'll engage you. It doesn't have any intelligence, except figuring out what gets the most clicks. The outrage stuff gets the most clicks, so it puts that at the top of the list."[27] "I think of it as civilization mind control," he says.[28]

One of this mysterious recommendation system's most powerful tools is topical affinity. If you enjoy cycling on the weekends and you search YouTube for videos about local trails, the system sees this, adds these details to the ever-lengthening biography it's writing about you, and begins to recommend things based on this latest intelligence: the top ten bicycles of the year, the best professional races, and so on. Over time, the recommendations become more extreme: dramatic crashes, death-defying stunt rides. What is the algorithm doing? Pulling users "toward ever more titillating variations on their interests."[29] If that's bikes or baseball, the impact isn't as worrisome. If it's politics, health, or other topics of similar gravity, the consequences can be detrimental to society.[30] If enough people spend enough of their time being machine-manipulated like this, it begins to change the culture. Our habits shape us. And when hate is our habit, we become something hideous, deformed creatures barely recognizable as humans. Our wrath makes us wraiths. Samuel James is right: The social internet's "algorithmic design to elicit our anger so as to command our attention is nothing less than a moral crisis."[31]

In a context where conflict is a core value, the most contentious participants are the most celebrated, which discourages

---

27. Klein, "How Technology Is Designed to Bring Out the Worst in Us."

28. Similarly, Fisher, *Chaos Machine*, 11, speaks of the people "who run the companies that run our minds."

29. Fisher, *Chaos Machine*, 109.

30. Studies have shown that the most engaging content on social media is what we might call "out-group animosity," that is, negative content posted by one political group about an opposing political group. See Martin, *Wolf in Their Pockets*, 115.

31. James, *Digital Liturgies*, 104.

calmness or kindness. What we celebrate, we cultivate, as the saying goes. The fast-paced flow of information online makes matters even more challenging. When topics appear and then give way to the next with such swiftness, it makes us think that we must speak to this important issue *now*. The problem is that almost never are my *first* thoughts my *best* thoughts. But in the kingdom called Digital, vehemence and urgency are king and queen. And the maxim of this kingdom, as Jonathan Haidt wryly observes, is "judge quickly and publicly, lest ye be judged for not judging, whoever it is that we are all condemning today."[32] Speak quickly and as nastily as possible, and you'll be noticed. Tension gets attention.

Media theorist Neil Postman argues that *forms* of public discourse regulate and even dictate what kind of *content* can issue from such forms. Postman gives the example of the primitive technology of smoke signals. "While I do not know exactly what content was once carried in the smoke signals of American Indians, I can safely guess that it did not include philosophical argument. Puffs of smoke are insufficiently complex to express ideas on the nature of existence, and even if they were not, a Cherokee philosopher would run short of either wood or blankets long before he reached his second axiom. You cannot use smoke to do philosophy. Its form excludes the content."[33] The form of social media, with its algorithmic design and its fast-paced flow, seems to me to exclude deep thought and patient, peaceable expression.[34] At the very least, we can say that it makes it much more difficult for us to heed the biblical directive: "Let every person be quick to hear, slow to speak, slow to anger" (Jas 1:19).

## CULTIVATING A HOLY CALMNESS

In the physical world, if I burst into someone else's house and begin yelling at them, probably my anger will get me arrested. But in

---

32. Haidt, *Anxious Generation*, 211.
33. Postman, *Amusing Ourselves to Death*, 6–7.
34. Vaidhyanathan, *Antisocial Media*, 8, draws a similar conclusion.

## Deathly (De)Vices

the digital world, starting arguments with strangers has become normal. The internet has recalibrated our sense of what is acceptable behavior.[35] Christ-followers need rhythms that remove us from this outrage factory and nurture what Jonathan Edwards calls "a holy calmness." Edwards writes, "The real strength of the good soldier of Jesus Christ is simply the steadfast maintenance of a holy calmness . . . sustained amidst all the storms, injuries, wrong behavior, and unexpected acts and events in this evil and unreasonable world."[36] "Whoever is slow to anger is better than the mighty, and he who rules his spirit than he who takes a city" (Prov 16:32).

Two surprisingly simple practices will contribute to a holy calmness: resting and reading. By "resting," really, I mean *sleeping*. Haidt details four foundational harms of the new phone-based childhood, one of which is sleep deprivation.[37] Every parent knows the struggle of getting children to bed on school nights, but this is indeed a parenting battle worth fighting. Sleep is vital for good performance in academics and in life. This is especially true during puberty, when the brain is racing with activity, changing far more rapidly than in years prior.[38] "Sleep-deprived teens cannot concentrate, focus, or remember as well as teens who get sufficient sleep. Their learning and their grades suffer. Their reaction times, decision making, and motor skills suffer, which elevates their risk of accidents. They are more irritable and anxious throughout the day, so their relationships suffer."[39] Teens require more sleep than adults—eight to nine hours per night—and when they don't get it, they experience impairment in virtually every sphere of activity. The predominant cause of sleep deprivation among teens is screen-based technologies in the bedroom. When a child scrolls

---

35. James, *Digital Liturgies*, 109.

36. Cited in McCracken, "How to Avoid Anger Overload in the Digital Age."

37. The others are social deprivation, attention fragmentation, and addiction. See Haidt, *Anxious Generation*, 113–41.

38. Haidt, *Anxious Generation*, 123.

39. Haidt, *Anxious Generation*, 123.

on social media or surfs the internet into the late night, the outrage factory energizes his anger while the sleep deprivation erodes his capacity for calmness and clear thinking.[40] The poor kid doesn't stand a chance. If little Johnny drinks this cocktail nightly, before long he'll begin to resemble Mr. Hyde, or the Hulk—always angry. When the kids *don't* snooze, everyone loses.

Of course, it's not just our children who need sufficient sleep. God wired *us* in such a way that our bodies require a rhythm of activity and inactivity, of work and rest, of labor and slumber. But many of us have convinced ourselves that we are the exceptions to the rule of rest. We aren't getting the nightly nourishment our bodies require, and it's affecting more than our beauty. In his article "The Science of Sleep," Michael Finkel reports that the average American today sleeps less than seven hours a night, about two hours less than a century ago.[41] Finkel contends that the culprit is electric light: televisions, tablets, and smartphones. Light at night hits the brake on the body's production of melatonin, the hormone that helps regulate biological rhythms. Thanks to the work of sleep researchers, we've learned that it takes only a small amount of light to throw off our rhythm.[42] Blue light, the kind we bathe in as we stare at our screens, has an especially disruptive effect. If it's 11:00 p.m. in New York but you've been immersed in screen-based technology all evening, your iPad may register 11:00 p.m., but the presence of artificial light has paused the internal tick-tocking of time by suppressing melatonin production. It's like you've been dragged westward to the internal equivalent of San Francisco time (8:00 p.m.).[43]

Underslept children and adults are more irrational, ill-tempered, even reckless.[44] But when the family receives with gratitude

---

40. See Walker, *Why We Sleep*, 145–52. He notes that insufficient sleep has been linked to aggression, bullying, and other behavioral problems in children across a range of ages.
41. Finkel, "Science of Sleep," 47.
42. Walker, *Why We Sleep*, 265–71.
43. Walker, *Why We Sleep*, 267–68.
44. DeYoung, *Glittering Vices*, 160, writes, "If we slept enough, practiced

## Deathly (De)Vices

God's good gift of sleep (Ps 127:2), it enhances the quality of every second we spend with our eyes open. When I'm well rested, I'm more likely to display Christ-like, self-sacrificing love toward my wife, and I'm calmer and more patient with my children. New Testament scholar D. A. Carson puts it in the most practical of terms: "We are whole, complicated beings: our physical existence is tied up to our spiritual well-being, to our mental outlook, to our relationship with others, including our relationship with God. Sometimes the godliest thing you can do in the universe is get a good night's sleep—not pray all night, but sleep."[45]

A second practice that will cultivate a holy calmness is reading. By "reading," I mean *reading old-fashioned books*: the type of book for which pine trees had to die, whose paper now can enact the tree's revenge by slicing your finger. If you can't feel the texture of the paper, then it's *not* the kind of reading I have in mind. For some people, reading a book seems archaic, like churning your own butter or baking your own bread. Why spend time baking bread when with the click of a box on an app I can have my groceries delivered to my front door? Why read a book when I can go to Google and absorb information quickly? What this way of thinking fails to consider is what we *lose* when we trade paper for pixels. Technology giveth, and technology taketh away, remember? What we lose is what some have called "the old linear thought process." "Calm, focused, undistracted, the linear mind is being pushed aside by a new kind of mind that wants and needs to take in and dole out information in short, disjointed, often overlapping bursts—the faster, the better."[46] In the now famous words from Nicholas Carr's classic, *The Shallows*, "What the Net seems to be doing is chipping away my capacity for concentration and contemplation. Whether I'm online or not, my mind now expects to take in information the way the Net distributes it: in a swiftly moving stream of particles.

---

silence and solitude each day, observed the Sabbath weekly, and took real retreats from work to breathe deeply and enjoy our natural surroundings, we might be less well-trained in wrath."

45. Cited in DeYoung, *Crazy Busy*, 97.
46. Carr, *Shallows*, 10.

Once I was a scuba diver in the sea of words. Now I zip along the surface like a guy on a Jet Ski."[47]

The internet has enticed many thoughtful people to slip into a perpetual state of distractedness, shallowness, and sharp-tonguedness. What we need is a tool with the ability to retrain our minds to focus on *one subject*, to have *deep thoughts*, and to have these thoughts without immediately *sharing* them far and wide. We need a piece of technology that will help us exercise the ministry of holding the tongue and controlling the typing fingers. The old-fashioned book does this. Reading a book is giving our best attention to someone else's best thoughts. When I'm reading a book, I'm *listening*, not speaking. Even if I disagree with the author, even if he or she angers me, it's much more difficult to express my anger in inappropriate ways. It's much more difficult to slander or smear. Where do I post? Whom do I tell? It's just me and the book. The act of reading an old-fashioned book is literally the act of being "quick to hear, slow to speak, slow to anger" (Jas 1:19).[48]

The internet shouts at me, "Go faster! Get louder! Do more!" Books whispers to me, "Be still. Be silent. Take your time."

---

47. Carr, *Shallows*, 6–7.
48. McCracken, *Wisdom Pyramid*, 119.

# 7

# Gluttony

## Taking Control of Our Information Intake

### DIALING IN OUR NUTRITION

TIM KELLER EXPLAINS, "BIBLICAL Christianity may be the most body-positive religion in the world. It teaches that God made matter and physical bodies and saw that it was all good (Genesis 1:31). It says that in Jesus Christ God himself actually took on a human body (which he still has in glorified form), and that someday he is going to give [his people] perfect, resurrected bodies."[1] In Christian theology, the body is not temporary or insignificant, the extreme espoused throughout the centuries by gnostic and other hyper-spiritual thinkers. Nor is the body ultimate, the opposite extreme communicated by our contemporary, sex-saturated society. The body is not to be idolized, nor is it to be ignored. Rather, as Dallas Willard says in his classic work on spiritual formation, "The body is to be regarded as holy, because it is owned and inhabited by God."[2]

---

1. Keller, *Meaning of Marriage*, 253. See also Lewis, *Mere Christianity*, 98: "Christianity is almost the only one of the great religions which thoroughly approves of the body."
2. Willard, *Renovation of the Heart*, 174.

The body, with its various capacities, is our tool for glorifying God (1 Cor 6:19–20); therefore, if we want to construct things for God, then we must care for our bodies. Stewarding our bodies well involves getting sufficient sleep (as we discussed in the previous chapter), ample physical activity, and proper nutrition. When my two now teenage sons were much younger, I attempted to teach them the basics of nutrition by using LEGO. (Yes, the ones Bricksie sold us.) The blue blocks represented protein, the red blocks were carbs, and the yellow blocks were fats. Once we learned about the macronutrients and the best sources of each, then we needed to learn about the right portions. We used a simple method. For example, a fist-size amount of chicken, a palm-size amount of almonds, and then fill in the rest of the plate with healthy carbs like fruits and veggies.

In addition to this very basic method, we had five guidelines, which we follow to this day. First, mostly avoid fast food. Robert Lustig, professor emeritus of pediatrics at the University of California, San Francisco, quips, "If the food comes in a wrapper, the wrapper has more health benefits than the food."[3] Second, prioritize family meals at the table, especially the evening meal. Third, remove sugary drinks from the home. Juice is marketed as a healthy option, but it's often loaded with sugar and is therefore a poor choice. The same is true of most energy drinks, sports drinks, and sodas. Fourth, limit dessert or sweet treats to once a week. Cutting out junk food altogether probably isn't sustainable over the long haul, but every successful nutrition plan in history has placed a limit on sugar consumption.[4] Finally, eat foods you can find in nature. When my sons were younger, they didn't understand the meaning of "highly processed," but when looking at a food, they knew to ask, "Does this look like something that could come straight from nature?" Egg? Yes. Apple? Yes. Bell pepper? Yes. Jell-O pudding? No. Gummy worm? No. Pretty sure those don't grow on trees. As a follow-up, they knew to ask, "Can I leave this food sitting on my shelf for weeks or even months without it

---

3. Lustig, *Fat Chance*, 206.
4. Lustig, *Fat Chance*, 117.

going bad?" If the answer is Yes, then it's probably not good for you. Whole foods like fruits and veggies go bad quickly compared to that Twinkie that's been sitting in your cupboard since the original *Ghostbusters* and probably could survive a nuclear attack.

## TRADITIONAL AND DIGITAL GLUTTONY

The sixth capital vice, gluttony, is a vice of excess. Traditionally, it refers to an excess related to eating: excessive portions of food or excessive pleasure derived from fine foods. The glutton might be an overeater or a food snob. Either way, the glutton hopes food will accomplish something that no creature comfort can. When feelings of emptiness threaten, the glutton reaches for the quick fix of chocolate, fine wine, a decadent meal out, a big bowl of mac and cheese, or a bag of chips, rather than reaching for resources that can satisfy him or her deep down.[5] The soul longs for something and the glutton responds by gorging the gut.

Food and drink are not bad things. Three times in the Gospels we find the phrase "The Son of Man came," followed by an explanation of why he came. "The Son of Man came not to be served but to serve, and to give his life as a ransom for many" (Matt 20:28; repeated in Mark 10:45). "The Son of Man came to seek and to save the lost" (Luke 19:10). And "the Son of Man came *eating and drinking*" (Matt 11:19). Jesus spent so much time socializing with tax collectors and sinners that some of his most vehement critics wrongly accused him of being a glutton and drunkard. He transformed water into wine—*good* wine (John 2:1–11). He turned a few loaves and fish into a pile of food large enough to serve a colossal crowd (e.g., Matt 14:13–21). When the resurrected Jesus appeared to his disciples, one of the first things he did was have a snack (Luke 24:36–43). Food and drink are not bad in themselves. They can't be, because the sinless Son of God enjoyed them. Gluttony is a vice of *excess*. I'm reminded of C. S. Lewis's discussion of the virtue Temperance, which he defines as "going the right length

---

5. DeYoung, *Glittering Vices*, 172.

## Gluttony

and no further."[6] "Going the right length" means not having too much, and—at the root of overindulgence—it means not putting too much hope in creature comforts, not looking to food and drink to satisfy us at the deepest level and with finality.

Where many expositions of the seven capital vices limit themselves to traditional gluttony, I want to focus on a modern variation of the vice: digital or information gluttony. Brett McCracken opens his book *The Wisdom Pyramid* with keen commentary on our cultural moment:

> Our world has more and more information, but less and less wisdom. More data; less clarity. More stimulation; less synthesis. More distraction; less stillness. More pontificating; less pondering. More opinion; less research. More speaking; less listening. More to look at; less to see. More amusements; less joy. There is more, but we are less. And we all feel it.[7]

The immensity of information available to us today is hard to fathom. British tech journalist Chris Stokel-Walker reports that in a three-month period in 2018, fifty-three million hours of footage went onto YouTube. To put that in perspective for you, watching non-stop, it would take a viewer until the year 8069 to watch all the YouTube uploads.[8] In 2020, there were forty times more bytes of data on the internet than there are stars in the observable universe. Some estimates suggest that by 2025, 463 exabytes of data will emerge each day online. That's the equivalent of 212,765,957 DVDs per day.[9] With so much to "eat," and with the bounty ever before us, it's unsurprising that so many of us have become information gluttons. And because so much of the information is

---

6. Lewis, *Mere Christianity*, 79. He goes on to say, "An individual Christian may see fit to give up all sorts of things for special reasons—marriage, or meat, or beer, or the cinema; but the moment he starts saying these things are bad in themselves, or looking down his nose at other people who do use them, he has taken the wrong turning."

7. McCracken, *Wisdom Pyramid*, 11.

8. Stokel-Walker, *YouTubers*, 13.

9. McCracken, *Wisdom Pyramid*, 27.

# Deathly (De)Vices

Twinkie-like, it's no wonder that so many of us have fat minds. Just as high-quality foods and the proper portions of them are necessary for physical health, so a sensible intake of reliable information is necessary for our intellectual, emotional, and spiritual health. The key, in a word, is *selectivity*. Or, in more spiritual terminology, *discernment*.

## TEST THE SPIRITS

Several of the documents contained in the NT were written, at least in part, to address false teaching, erroneous ideas, *bad information*. First and Second John fit within this category. Probably, John wrote his letters in the closing decades of the first century, making these among the latest documents of the NT.[10] At the time of writing, it's possible that John was the last living apostle. Imagine living at this moment in history. You know the stories and the powerful deeds of Jesus, not because you knew him personally, but because you've heard about Jesus via the apostles' teaching. *They* are the eyewitnesses; *they* walked with the resurrected Lord; *they* received the truth from the mouth of Jesus himself. This period of history was very different from ours in terms of the flow of information: no publishing industry, no podcasts, no smartphones or social media, no information glut. People didn't have easy access to theological sources, at least not to written sources. So the living, walking sources were all the more important. But slowly, the apostles began to disappear, until only John remained—and he wasn't the strapping young lad he once was. The early Christians must have wondered, "Where will we turn for answers when the last apostle is gone? Who will teach us the truth?" Late first-century believers stood on the brink of a new era, a time of transition from the apostles to the next generation of church leaders. During this time, several erroneous ideas arose, some that were similar to the apostles' teaching, and others that were radically different.[11] This

---

10. On questions of authorship and date, see Marshall, *Epistles of John*, 42–8; Yarbrough, *1–3 John*, 5–17.

11. Jobes, *1, 2 and 3 John*, 30.

influx of new ideas caused many in the church to become confused, uncertain. John, moved by a sense of pastoral responsibility, wrote his first and second letters to address this very problem.[12]

In 1 John 4:1, John writes to the church, "Beloved, do not believe every spirit, but test the spirits to see whether they are from God, for many false prophets have gone out into the world." The first imperative in v. 1 is "do not believe every spirit." This is noteworthy. In the contemporary church, we spend much of our time (in sermons and small group discussions) talking about the things we ought to believe, which of course is a suitable endeavor, but let us not forget about belief's bedfellow. John understands that *belief* and *disbelief* travel together, like two compartments of the one suitcase. On the zipper side of the suitcase are all the ideas we do believe, and on the strappy-thing side are all the ideas we do not believe. If I am convinced that $2 + 2 = 4$, then necessarily I do not believe that $2 + 2 = 5$. The same is true in the realm of theology. To believe certain claims about God, God's world, and our place within the world means that we must refuse to believe certain other claims. If I am convinced of Jesus' divinity, then necessarily I must refuse to believe that Jesus was merely a good teacher. As Sherlock Holmes would say, "Elementary, my dear Watson!" Indeed this is elementary, but in a society that worships a caricature of the virtue called Tolerance, we need these rudimentary reminders that true belief is ballsy: It requires us to say, "I do *not* believe that." Albeit, always with gentleness and respect.

The second command of v. 1 is "test the spirits." The verb *dokimazō* is the sort of term we would expect to find in a Sherlock Holmes story. It means "to make a critical examination." John insists that we inspect the spirits. "Spirits" is an interesting choice of words. It reminds me of the words the Ghost of Jacob Marley utters to Ebenezer Scrooge in *A Christmas Carol*: "You will be haunted

---

12. Whereas 2 John is more about stopping the spread of falsehood, 3 John is concerned with supporting the spread of the truth. God, in his providence, saw to it that both bite-sized letters were preserved through the centuries, so that the church would know both her defensive and her offensive role.

## Deathly (De)vices

by Three Spirits."[13] Rather kind of Marley, I've always thought, to let Scrooge know exactly how many spirits were on the way, and furthermore to tell him precisely when each spirit would appear. You and I are not so fortunate. John assumes that we will be visited by spirits, though he doesn't recount their number or time of arrival, leaving us in desperate curiosity.

By "spirit" John doesn't mean specter or phantom; rather, he means a person carrying a message. Notice how he clarifies the word *spirit* in the final part of v. 1: "Test the spirits to see whether they are from God, for many *false prophets* have gone out into the world." John's warning to the church concerns false teachers, flesh-and-blood people. Why, then, does he refer to them as "spirits"? Because he wants us to see that behind every *person* is a *power*. Already in his letter, John has divided the people of planet Earth into two groups: the children of God and the children of the devil (3:10). The children of God have Holy Spirit power. The children of the devil are under Satan's power, doing his bidding, planting his lies. In C. S. Lewis's space trilogy, the main character, Dr. Ransom, elucidates the point: "There are spirits and spirits you know . . . . A thing might be a spirit and not good for you."[14] Therefore, we must "test" before trusting. Test every preacher and politician, every author and filmmaker, every YouTube influencer and game developer.

The foremost question in the test, John says, is the Christological question: What does this person claim about the identity and ministry of Jesus?[15] "By this you know the Spirit of God: every spirit that confesses that Jesus Christ has come in the flesh is from God, and every spirit that does not confess Jesus is not from God"

---

13. Dickens, *Christmas Carol*, 18.
14. Lewis, *Perelandra*, 80.
15. Additionally, John develops (2) the biblical question (Is this person's message consistent with the apostles' teaching?) and (3) the moral question (Does this person's life showcase the transformative power of the gospel?). To these we could add (4) the communal question (What do other believers in my Christian community think of this person's message?) and (5) the historical question (Is this person's message consistent with the faithful expositions of Scripture we find throughout Christian history?).

(1 John 4:2–3a). In his second letter, John reiterates the centrality of Christ and then explains what the church must do when a messenger fails this all-important test:

> For many deceivers have gone out into the world, those who do not confess the coming of Jesus Christ in the flesh. Such a one is the deceiver and the antichrist. Watch yourselves, so that you may not lose what we have worked for, but may win a full reward. Everyone who goes on ahead and does not abide in the teaching of Christ, does not have God. Whoever abides in the teaching has both the Father and the Son. If anyone comes to you and does not bring this teaching, do not receive him into your house or give him any greeting, for whoever greets him takes part in his wicked works. (2 John 7–11)

I'd wager all the bourbon in Kentucky on this guess: One of the words from that passage that made your mind fidgety is "antichrist." In his first letter, John asserts, "Many antichrists have come" (1 John 2:18). Books and films have conditioned us to expect *the Antichrist*, some mega-villain who will rise to power at the end of time. I know it makes for an entertaining movie, but this is not what the Bible teaches on the subject. In Scripture, the only occurrences of the term *antichrist* are in 1 and 2 John, and John is unequivocal on two matters. First, there are *many* antichrists, not one. Second, they exist in the *present*, not merely in the future. "Antichrist" is best understood as a label that applies to deceptive individuals, people who once were affiliated with the Christian community, but who now have "progressed" in their belief and teaching to the point that John considers them to be *anti-Jesus*.[16]

With this type of person in mind, John says to the church, "Do not receive him into your house or give him any greeting, for whoever greets him takes part in his wicked works" (2 John 10–11). True belief is ballsy, remember? It requires us to say, "I do *not* believe that." And at times the message is so detestable that we are expected to say, "You can't bring that into my house." Toward

---

16. Jobes, *1, 2, and 3 John*, 123, following the interpretation of Didymus the Blind.

## Deathly (De)Vices

some information, Scripture summons us to be inhospitable. Bear in mind that in John's first-century context the Christians met in homes. They relied on the few wealthy people in the congregation who owned homes to provide meeting space for their regular times of worship. In this context, "receiving [the deceivers] into your house" would have meant supplying them with a ready-made audience.[17] John isn't calling us to be disrespectful or hateful toward the deceivers themselves.[18] He is, however, insisting that we avoid their influence personally, and that we do what is within our power to curb their influence on the communal level. We mustn't provide a non-critical ear, encourage them in their propaganda, provide them with a platform, or otherwise support their "ministry." As NT scholar Karen Jobes reminds us, "Social gestures are not always spiritually neutral acts."[19] In John's day, something so simple as opening the door of one's home would have been considered taking part in wicked works (v. 11).

In some ways, John's first-century readers had it harder than we do today. As we've noted, they didn't have access to theological sources the way we do. They didn't yet have the books of the Bible all collected into one, handsome volume. The truth of God's word is far more accessible today, at least in my home country, and for this we should be thankful. But in other ways, I think John's first-century readers had it easier than we do today. Then, detecting a deceiver was less complicated, because the deceiver was *unmediated*. It was a flesh-and-blood person standing at the door of the house. Now, most deceivers don't enter through our doors; they enter through our devices. They don't need you to unlock the door and let them in; all they need is for you to unlock your device and let down your guard.

---

17. Thielman, *Theology of the New Testament*, 560. Brown, *Epistles of John*, 676, says that John prohibits "the reception of the false teachers at the place and on the occasion where their teaching could be spread."

18. Second Timothy, another polemical letter of the NT, calls for the patient and gentle correction of false teachers, with the hope that they will repent of their devilish ways (2 Tim 2:24–26).

19. Jobes, *1, 2, and 3 John*, 272.

## TESTING THE SPIRITS IN THE DIGITAL SPHERE

After Marley's Ghost announces Scrooge's haunting itinerary, Scrooge walks to his window. The air over the city "was filled with phantoms, wandering hither and thither in restless haste, and moaning as they went."[20] The scene serves as an apt analogy for the internet: countless spirits swarming, never still, never silent. In modern parlance, John's letters teach us that we should make a critical examination of these spirits on the internet and that we should be cautious about the messages we affirm, the people we follow, and the channels to which we subscribe. Social *media* gestures are not always spiritually neutral acts. But before we think about how to properly test the spirits online, we must first understand how *the medium itself* complicates things for us.

In his book *The Death of Expertise*, Tom Nichols states the problem plainly: "Some of the smartest people on earth have a significant presence on the Internet. Some of the stupidest people on the planet, however, reside just one click away on the next page or hyperlink."[21] Nichols continues:

> The freedom to post anything online floods the public square with bad information and half-baked thinking. The Internet lets a billion flowers bloom, and most of them stink, including everything from the idle thoughts of random bloggers and the conspiracy theories of cranks all the way to the sophisticated campaigns of disinformation conducted by groups and governments. Some of the information on the Internet is wrong because of sloppiness, some of it is wrong because well-meaning people just don't know any better, and some of it is wrong because it was put there out of greed or even sheer malice. The medium itself, without comment or editorial intervention, displays it all with equal speed.[22]

---

20. Dickens, *Christmas Carol*, 19.
21. Nichols, *Death of Expertise*, 108.
22. Nichols, *Death of Expertise*, 108–9.

## Deathly (De)Vices

A vast amount of the information available online hasn't had to pass the muster of gatekeepers. To publish a book in the traditional way, an author first writes a book proposal for a publisher. If the publisher sees merit in the project, and agrees to publish it, then the author gets to work, researching and writing—for months or maybe years. Once the author finishes the manuscript, it then goes to a team of editors. Only after much scrutiny and (usually) some revision does the book become available to the public. The process is similar if a person aspires to publish his or her thoughts in a traditional journal or periodical. If an author submits an article to an academic journal, it goes through a peer-review process: other scholars in the field read it carefully, recommending that the piece be rejected, revised, or published. Gatekeepers galore. Of course, processes like these don't guarantee the absence of error, but they diminish the likelihood of error's presence. In contrast, the process for publishing content online is as simple as: (1) get a device; (2) get a social media platform; and (3) start sharing your ideas with the world. No gatekeepers. If such a person gains enough attention, he or she might even become known as an "expert" or a "thought leader." Thanks to the internet, we all think we're experts in everything. We're not.

True expertise is a combination of education, talent, experience, and peer affirmation.[23] Formal training is the first and most obvious mark of expert status, though it's only a start. Talent separates those who have gained credentials from those who rise to the top of their field of study. A brilliant law student who freezes in front of a jury can get only so far. Experience is another important factor. Experts remain engaged in their field, continually improve their skills, learn from their missteps, and over the span of their careers develop a somewhat intangible intuition. Experienced law enforcement officers have an instinct for trouble that their younger colleagues lack. Veteran teachers find difficult students less intimidating. A fourth mark of true experts is their acceptance of evaluation by other experts in their field. Mechanisms like peer review, board certification, and professional associations ensure

---

23. Based on the discussion in Nichols, *Death of Expertise*, 28–39.

high standards of work and enhance social trust. When you take the elevator to the top floor of a tall building, the certificate posted in that elevator assures you that a civic authority, relying on a guild of engineers, have inspected this moving box and know, with as much certainty as anyone can, that you'll be safe. That certificate is much more reassuring than a sign that simply says, "Good luck up there."[24]

Medical doctors, engineers, and airline pilots are experts. If I need heart surgery, I want a surgeon who went to a reputable med school, not some guy who's watched a thousand episodes of *ER* and has a really popular podcast. Experts aren't right about everything, but they are more often right than wrong on matters related to their fields. Within these parameters, they are more *reliable*. This, then, is the first caution sign as we manage the information glut: (1) Not everyone online is an expert.

Our second caution sign is: (2) When online, the sources from which we choose have been chosen for us. We tend to think of the internet as the world's largest library and the act of googling as akin to perusing the aisles of said library, making a careful selection from among the best sources available to us. This assumption is mistaken, and in two ways. First, not all the sources we encounter in the digital sphere should be considered "best" or even "good."[25] In the words Davy Crockett once spoke to Andrew Jackson, some of it doesn't even make good nonsense. Refer to caution sign one. Second, the sources in front of us have been algorithmically arranged. When we do "research" online it doesn't feel as if our "findings" have been especially selected to feed our particular appetites, to keep us engaged, but this is precisely what has transpired. "A search for information will cough up whatever algorithm is at

24. Nichols, *Death of Expertise*, 35–36.
25. As a case in point, *false* information moves *fastest* and *furthest* online. As the saying goes, "A lie can travel around the world and back again while the truth is lacing up its boots." False news is more novel, and people are more likely to share novel information. Who cares if it's good or bad, right or wrong? What matters is that I'm the *first* to post about it. See Dizikes, "Study: On Twitter, False News Travels Faster Than True Stories"; Martin, *Wolf in Their Pockets*, 89.

## Deathly (De)Vices

work in a search engine, usually provided by for-profit companies using criteria that are largely opaque to the user."[26] Google's mission is to "organize the world's information and make it universally accessible and useful."[27] What Google means by "organizing" actually is a process of customizing what we see based on data it's milked from us. Remember the designation "data cows"? Rather than entering the grandest library with the freedom to roam and to access all the information therein, going online is more like being trapped in one aisle of the library. Even worse, it's like certain "books" from that aisle are being pushed off the shelves at us—the ones *they* want us to read, whoever *they* are.[28]

General cautions in place, we may now turn to the primary matter: testing those innumerable spirits that speak to us in the digital sphere. Of this buffet that has been placed before us, with each dish averring that it is the super source we need, how do we determine which ones to consume, metabolize, recommend, and share with others? World-renowned scientist and committed Christian Francis Collins suggests four criteria.[29] The first is *integrity*. Does this individual or institution represent honesty and moral uprightness? Do they have a reputation for fairness? How have they handled difficult subjects or situations?

The second criterion is *competence*. Does this person have real competence in the relevant domain? Beware professional athletes pontificating on political science and celebrities waxing eloquent on nutrition. Every opinion is *not* as good as every other. Collins tells of a friend who gave him a coffee mug with the caption "Do not confuse your Google search with my medical degree." He also tells of a neighborhood close to his home where he once saw

---

26. Nichols, *Death of Expertise*, 110. See also Song, *Restless Devices*, 39–43.

27. Cited in Song, *Restless Devices*, 40.

28. Collins, *Road to Wisdom*, 58, speaks similarly of social media: "Here's the bottom line: if you are currently utilizing social media as your main source of information about what's happening in the world, you are missing some really important events, and you are almost certainly being unwittingly manipulated by forces in the dark corners of the internet."

29. See Collins, *Road to Wisdom*, 185–89.

a Halloween display: in a fake graveyard, one of the gravestones read, "I did my own research."[30] True expertise matters!

Third, when making trust decisions online, we should consider the *humility* of the source. Does this writer or speaker possess an honest recognition of his or her limitations? Does he know *what he does not know*? Hearing a person say with sincerity, "I'm not the best person to address *this* matter" provides a reason to trust her even more on *that* matter, the one that falls within her area of expertise. If the passion of one's conviction matches the depth of his investigation, this is a good sign. Conversely, if a person claims 100 percent certainty about every subject under the sun, run, all the while remembering Christopher Hitchen's rule, sometimes called Hitchen's Razor: "What can be asserted without evidence can also be dismissed without evidence."[31]

The final factor is a tricky one. Collins labels it *aligned values*. Each one of us has certain life experiences, social groupings, and attitudes toward other communities that may be positive or negative. Our likelihood of accepting a source of information as trustworthy depends, to a degree, on whether or not we think that source is one with which we share aligned values. If a person's worldview is very similar to my own, then I am more inclined to trust his words. But we have to be careful here, remembering the importance of the other criteria. Aligned values is no substitute for actual proficiency. If given the choice between boarding a plane piloted by a devout Christian who's practically memorized *Top Gun* and another plane piloted by a vehement atheist who actually went to flight school, I'm flying Atheist Airlines every time.

To overtly (and covertly) religious messages, we should apply the apostle John's test: What does this person or community claim about the identity and ministry of Jesus? Always, this is the place to start. For the wider range of messages we encounter online—"Buy this product," "Drink that supplement," "Enroll your kids in this type of school," "Avoid that vaccination"—Collins provides some much-needed help. With more information available to us

---

30. Collins, *Road to Wisdom*, 187.
31. Cited in Collins, *Road to Wisdom*, 61.

than ever before, it's more important than ever for us to implement a rational scheme for sifting through it all.

## FEAR-INDUCING AND FAITH-INDUCING SOURCES

While working on this project, I participated in a learning cohort organized by the Center for Pastor Theologians. Our group spent a year exploring the formational impact of digital technologies. At the outset of the journey, each participant completed an introductory questionnaire, which included the question "What word(s) would you use to describe how you feel when you're online?" The top three answers were *distracted*, *overfed*, and *frustrated*.[32] What we eat affects the way we feel. If you don't believe me, try eating only Twinkies for a month and see how it affects your mood. On second thought, don't do this experiment: you might die. When we gorge ourselves on Google, social media, and other digital junk food, it has a negative influence on our intellectual, emotional, and spiritual health. It makes us *angry*, *afraid*, and *anxious*.

A healthy diet involves more than subtraction; it's also about addition. We must decrease the intake of Twinkies and increase the intake of veggies. In Matt 6:26–30, Jesus preaches on anxiety, saying:

> Look at the birds of the air: they neither sow nor reap nor gather into barns, and yet your heavenly Father feeds them. Are you not of more value than they? And which of you by being anxious can add a single hour to his span of life? And why are you anxious about clothing? Consider the lilies of the field, how they grow: they neither toil nor spin, yet I tell you, even Solomon in all his glory was not arrayed like one of these. But if God so clothes the grass of the field, which today is alive and tomorrow is thrown into the oven, will he not much more clothe you, O you of little faith?

---

32. Followed by *scattered*, *tethered*, *hurried*, and *tired*.

## GLUTTONY

Jesus invites us to see the evidence of God's provision that is all around us. "Look at the birds of the air." "Consider the lilies of the field." He invites us to feast on *faith*-inducing sources. Most of us spend hours every day with *fear*-inducing sources: swiping and scrolling on social media, skimming the headlines, listening to talking heads. We spend relatively little time with faith-inducing sources. The two great faith-inducing sources are Scripture and nature.[33] In Scripture, we encounter our Maker. As we read these words of life, God reveals himself, his plan for the world he fashioned, where *he* is taking things—despite what the headlines suggest about who is at the helm of this world. In nature, too, we learn something of the ways of God, in the same way that we learn about Vincent van Gogh by studying his paintings or become better acquainted with Christopher Nolan by watching his films. "[God] not only gives us a literal book we can read and preach; he gives us a book we can see, hear, smell, touch, and taste—a book that runs through our hands like warm sand, rushes over us like a cold mountain waterfall, trickles down our mouth like juice from a peach. All of it bears his mark. Nature is one big, beautiful symphony that is always playing, if only we take out our earbuds long enough to listen."[34]

In recent years, I've discovered a pattern in myself. Every November–December I grab a Wendell Berry book off my shelf. I think it has to do with the weather changing. In Florida, *finally* we're beginning to feel some semblance of coolness in the mornings, which makes me want to venture outside more than usual. If you know anything about Wendell Berry, then you know that one simply must read him *outdoors*, *away* from technology, *in* nature. Berry is an articulate appreciator of nature, as he demonstrates

---

33. For a book-length treatment of these, I highly recommend McCracken, *Wisdom Pyramid*. McCracken expands the discussion to include six sources of wisdom: the Bible (the base of the Wisdom Pyramid); the church; nature; books; beauty; and technology (the peak or "use-sparingly" portion of the pyramid). McCracken rightly points out that many homes today have flipped the pyramid, with the internet and social media occupying the foundation, and the Bible occupying the "use-sparingly" peak.

34. McCracken, *Wisdom Pyramid*, 104–5.

throughout his corpus, and especially in his poem "The Peace of Wild Things."

> When despair for the world grows in me
> And I wake in the night at the least sound
> in fear of what my life and my children's lives may be,
> I go and lie down where the wood drake
> rests in his beauty on the water, and the great heron feeds.
> I come into the peace of wild things
> who do not tax their lives with forethought
> of grief. I come into the presence of still water.
> And I feel above me the day-blind stars
> waiting with their light. For a time
> I rest in the grace of the world, and am free.[35]

Add some new sources to the diet: look at the birds; consider the lilies; experience the peace of wild things.

---

35. Berry, *Peace of Wild Things and Other Poems*, 25.

# 8

# Lust

From *I Love Lucy* to Full Frontal Nudity

## POOR TIMES

IN 2024, EMMA STONE won best actress for her role as Bella Baxter in the dark, steampunk film *Poor Things*. I like Emma Stone as an actress, but I haven't seen the film—and I don't intend to. According to IMDb, *Poor Things* is rated R for "strong and pervasive sexual content, graphic nudity, disturbing material" and more.[1] The material was so "disturbing," in fact, that the British Board of Film Classification required editing before the film could be released in the UK. The most controversial scene involved two young boys watching Bella Baxter work as a prostitute.[2] In the summer of 2024, my family flew internationally. One of the in-flight movies was *Poor Things*. At one point, a passenger seated a few rows in front of us started watching it. I panicked. I had read enough about the film to recognize it and to know what it contains. My adolescent sons were seated right next to me, with a clear view of the screen that soon would teem with "disturbing material." What was a father to do? Tell his sons to close their eyes for the next two hours? I felt powerless.

1. IMDb, "Poor Things."
2. Bergeson, "'Poor Things' Sex Scene Re-Edited for U.K. Release."

## Deathly (De)Vices

Providentially, the passenger in front us quickly pivoted to a different movie—and my heart went back to beating.

This in-flight moment represents what some have called the "pornification" of culture.[3] Had the passenger in front of us not pivoted, my sons would have *become* the two young boys watching Bella Baxter work as a prostitute, and simply by being on an airplane. When I was a kid, my dad watched reruns of *The Andy Griffith Show*, and my mom's favorite haunt was *I Love Lucy*. Occasionally I watched the show with her, and I remember thinking, "Why does this married couple sleep in separate beds?" If you're unfamiliar with the classic sitcom, when *I Love Lucy* premiered in the early '50s, Lucy and Desi slept in twin beds. In those days, television producers were far more conservative.[4] When the real-world Lucille Ball became pregnant, the story-world Lucy had to hide her pregnancy from the audience. Finally, when hiding became impossible, the writers approached the subject, though they banned the word *pregnant*. Instead, Lucy was "expecting," a word more fitting for a woman never seen in bed with her husband. Any child to grace such a home must surely arrive by some mythological means: a long-legged bird delivering always-peaceful babies by night, perhaps.

In the '50s and '60s, two of the most popular television shows in America were *I Love Lucy* and *The Andy Griffith Show*. In 2017, *Game of Thrones* topped the list.[5] We've gone from Lucy and Desi sleeping in separate beds and the varied but always wholesome occurrences of Mayberry to full frontal nudity. And the problem is not limited to the shows and films of our cultural moment. Some social media platforms allow explicit sexual content that falls into the traditional category of pornography, though every social media platform allows sexually suggestive content.[6] Popular song

---

3. See, for example, Barton, *Pornification of America*; Grant, *Divine Sex*.
4. See Sorkin, *Being the Ricardos*.
5. Smith, *(Un)Intentional*, 39.
6. Martin, *Wolf in Their Pockets*, 156, points out that Twitter, Snapchat, and Reddit allow pornographic content. The problems with social media extend to the way algorithms foster certain types of communities. See, for example,

lyrics are hypersexualized. As the feminist author Naomi Wolf has put it, porn has indeed become "the wallpaper of our lives."[7]

## DIVINE SEX

We should begin our reflection on the final capital vice—lust—by elucidating the intrinsic *goodness* of this bare thing called sex. I doubt this would be the default understanding in our churches. Certainly it wasn't the impression of the church-grown young'uns in the Bible Belt, from which I hail. The church of my adolescent years didn't mention sex often. And when it did, always it was mentioned softly and with a negative slant. Sex simply was one of those things we weren't supposed to do, like drugs and all other kinds of devilry. Even sexual desire was treated as something shameful and sinister. The message ingrained in my teenage self was: "Sex: Don't do it. And if you find yourself wanting to do it, then don't talk about that. Cage all aspects of your sexual self until you get married. Because that's what good Christians do." I can see now how this summa of sexuality misses the mark. It often leads young men and women in the church to outright rebellion. Having no alacrity for the church's "sex-is-bad" view, they embrace the culture's "sex-is-god" view. Their lived confession becomes: "There is only one god, and pleasure is his prophet." Other times, this summa afflicts men and women with a sex negativity that lingers throughout their married years. "If sex was so bad before, then why does it suddenly become good at the moment of marriage? What if it's still shameful, gross, disgusting, sinful?"

In his book *Non-Toxic Masculinity*, Zachary Wagner says what I wish someone in my church would have said to my adolescent self: "Your pursuit of sex is a pursuit of something good. Your desire for sex is good. The desire isn't bad before marriage and good after marriage."[8] Sex itself is good. In fact, I'll go a step

---

Thomas, "How Instagram's Algorithm Connects and Promotes Pedophile Network."

7. Wolf, "Porn Myth."
8. Wagner, *Non-Toxic Masculinity*, 81.

## Deathly (De)vices

further. God loves sex. Of course he does. He invented the thing. Humanity didn't create sex. It's not as if Adam and Eve were frolicking in Eden one day, naked and unashamed, when suddenly she tripped, he fell, and by sheer happenstance things all fell into place: "Eureka!" Sex is God's invention. It is *divine, from God.*

Since God is the designer of sex, it is his prerogative to determine the context in which his good gift is to be enjoyed, which he does: one man and one woman committed exclusively to each other for life.[9] Why would God restrict sex to the context of marriage? Because as the designer, he knows just how powerful an invention sex is.

Helen Fisher is a biological anthropologist and an expert on the science of romantic love. Her book *Anatomy of Love* is a contemporary classic, and her TED talks on the subject have millions of views. Writing from a purely academic perspective, Fisher explains,

> Romantic love is an addiction: a perfectly wonderful addiction when it's going well, and a perfectly horrible addiction when it's going poorly. . . . Romantic love is an obsession. It possesses you. You lose your sense of self. You can't stop thinking about another human being. . . . The main characteristics of romantic love are craving: an intense craving to be with a particular person, not just sexually, but emotionally.[10]

Fisher expounds the neuroscience behind her conclusions. When we become infatuated with someone, she says, this has a surprisingly powerful influence on the brain. It impacts the same brain centers as cocaine, and with similar intensity. When you have sex with someone, in addition to the physical attachment, there's a spiritual-emotional attachment that develops during the experience.[11] Sexual climax releases a rush of neurotransmitters and hormones, deepening the attachment, strengthening the addiction.

---

9. For a book-length defense of this view, see Jones, *Faithful.*
10. Cited in Grant, *Divine Sex*, 39.
11. Fisher points to that unique sense of cosmic union a couple experiences during and after sex. See the discussion in Grant, *Divine Sex*, 40–41.

## LUST

In other words, there's no such thing as casual sex. You can't have a casual sexual partner in the same way that you can't have a casual drug problem, a casual cocaine addiction. It's scientifically nonsensical to think that we can sleep with as many people as we want and end these sexual relationships with no harm, no pain. Our brains aren't wired that way.

From a Christian perspective, the neuroscience makes perfect sense. Sex is a God-given gift with a God-given context: one man, one woman, addicted to each other for life. By divine design, sex is the most powerful way to give, not merely your body, but *your entire self*, to another human being. It is God's appointed way for a man and woman to say to one another, "I belong completely, permanently, and exclusively to you."[12] There's an integrity associated with the biblical sexual ethic. The Christian man says, "I won't give myself to a woman *physically* until I'm ready to give myself to her *emotionally, mentally, financially*, and in every possible way."[13] As C. S. Lewis puts it,

> The Christian idea of marriage is based on Christ's words that a man and wife are to be regarded as a single organism—for that is what the words "one flesh" would be in modern English. And the Christians believe that when He said this He was not expressing a sentiment but stating a fact—just as one is stating a fact when one says that a lock and its key are one mechanism, or that a violin and a bow are one musical instrument. The inventor of the human machine was telling us that its two halves, the male and the female, were made to be combined together in pairs, not simply on the sexual level, but totally combined. The monstrosity of sexual intercourse outside marriage is that those who indulge in it are trying to isolate one kind of union (the sexual) from all the other

---

12. Keller, *Meaning of Marriage*, 257.
13. Pearcey, *Love Thy Body*, 137: "You should become naked and vulnerable physically only when you are ready to become naked and vulnerable with your whole self."

kinds of union which were intended to go along with it and make up the total union.[14]

Ultimately, fidelity between husband and wife is a tangible testimony to God's unfailing fidelity toward his people. Christians testify *with our bodies*.[15] Maybe the Puritan pastor William Perkins was right when he insisted that marital sex is as spiritual as preaching.[16] But we must also admit that sexuality—in a fallen world—is expressed in many ways that ignore God's good design and that fail to tell the truth of his faithfulness.

## LUST: DEHUMANIZING PEOPLE

> You have heard that it was said, "You shall not commit adultery." But I say to you that everyone who looks at a woman with lustful intent has already committed adultery with her in his heart. If your right eye causes you to sin, tear it out and throw it away. For it is better that you lose one of your members than that your whole body be thrown into hell. And if your right hand causes you to sin, cut it off and throw it away. For it is better that you lose one of your members than that your whole body go into hell. (Matt 5:27–30)

The Sermon on the Mount is the closest thing to a manifesto that Jesus ever uttered. It's Jesus' own description of who his followers ought to *be* and what we ought to *do*. In chapter 5 of the sermon, a very noticeable pattern emerges. Time and time again, Jesus says, "You have heard that it was said . . . . But I say to you . . . ." In each case, he references the OT—either a specific verse or some interpretation of it—and then he helps his disciples see the deeper demand of these words.

In Matt 5:27, Jesus references the seventh commandment, "You shall not commit adultery." The rabbis limited this commandment to the physical realm. Thus, they had a conveniently narrow

---

14. Lewis, *Mere Christianity*, 104–5.
15. Jones, *Faithful*, 58.
16. Pearcey, *Toxic War on Masculinity*, 78–79.

## Lust

definition of sexual sin and a conveniently broad definition of purity.[17] "If I do not *touch* another person's spouse, then I am sexually pure," they thought. Jesus introduces the mental realm. "While it's good that you haven't *touched* another person's spouse," he says, "if you have *contemplated* him or her in a sexual way, then you have committed adultery in your heart." *Contemplate* is the right word, I think. When I contemplate a subject, I don't merely look; I *look at length*. Jesus warns us, not about a passing glance, a brief notice that someone is physically attractive. He warns us about looking "with lustful intent" (v. 28). Lust is in a man who notices a beautiful woman, imagines himself with her in some sexual way, purposes to take from her what he wants.[18]

Lust involves objectification, dehumanization. It "strips sexual pleasure-seeking down to individual gratification, apart from a love relationship to a person."[19] Strictly speaking, lust doesn't want a woman; it wants an experience for which a woman is the necessary apparatus.[20] Lust craves *it* rather than cherishing *her*. This is why the dancers in "gentleman's clubs"—what a preposterous title—use stage names.[21] A woman's real name would be an obstacle to the objectification that lust needs.[22] The best way to empty a gentleman's club would be to begin introducing the dancers using their real names and sharing a few details of their real lives. "This

---

17. Stott, *Message of the Sermon on the Mount*, 67.

18. Carson, *Jesus' Sermon on the Mount and His Confrontation with the World*, 55, writes, "This is not a prohibition of the normal attraction which exists between men and women, but of the deep-seated lust which consumes and devours, which in imagination attacks and rapes, which mentally contemplates and commits adultery."

19. DeYoung, *Glittering Vices*, 196.

20. Lewis, *Four Loves*, 94.

21. Fradd's comment is apropos: "A hundred years ago in England, if you were going to a gentleman's club, it was understood that you were going to a private upper-class establishment where you could relax, read, play parlor games, dine, and gossip with others of your class. Today in the United States, if you say you are going to a gentleman's club, it is assumed that you will be paying to see a striptease in a low-lit bar that smells like urinals and hopelessness" (*Porn Myth*, 31).

22. DeYoung, *Glittering Vices*, 197.

## Deathly (De)vices

is Suzy. Her mom was an alcoholic. She has two daughters. Suzy hopes to go to college someday and aspires eventually to become a nurse."

Commenting on v. 28, Wagner points out, "[Jesus] did not say, 'Therefore, never look at a woman.' Nor did he say, 'Women, make sure men don't look lustfully at you.' The responsibility remains with men to look at women differently. We must remind men that all women are worthy of dignity and respect because *they are human.*"[23] Upon noticing a woman's beauty, the far more gentlemanly thing—indeed, the godly thing—is to praise the Creator of all beauty. In my morning devotions, often I use collections of prayers. One of the collections I frequent is *Every Moment Holy*, which contains prayers that help the reader think theologically about, quite literally, every moment of life. It includes a prayer for leaving on holiday, for doing laundry, for the keeping of bees, and for feasting with friends. It even has a prayer for seeing a beautiful person:

> Lord, I praise you for divine beauty reflected in the form of this person. Now train my heart so that my response to their beauty would not be twisted downward into envy or desire, but would instead be directed upward in worship of you, their Creator—as was your intention for all such beauty before the breaking of the world.[24]

Having established the problem of lust, Jesus goes on to tell us what we must *do* about our lust. In vv. 29–30, he speaks of tearing out the eye and cutting off the hand. This is not a call to self-mutilation, though certain Christians from history have taken it that way. Origen of Alexandria castrated himself. I don't recommend that. We shouldn't take these words literally, and we know this because to take them literally wouldn't actually solve the problem. If I tear out my right eye, still I have my left eye with which to lust. Problem *not* solved. Jesus speaks figuratively here. His point is that we must be prepared to take extreme measures to combat sin.

---

23. Wagner, *Non-Toxic Masculinity*, 154 (emphasis added).
24. McKelvey, *Every Moment Holy*, 249.

## LUST

He chooses the right eye and the right hand because these were the most significant. To paraphrase, "Be rid of that which is most important to you, if it leads you to sin."

The fight against sin begins on the battlefield of the heart, as the prayer from *Every Moment Holy* acknowledges: Lord, "train our hearts." But this deeply theological battle is at the same time an intensely practical one. Jesus insists that we block the road that leads us to the locale of lust. We take very practical steps like this in other areas of life. If I struggle with overspending, then I cut up the credit card. If I struggle with eating, then I don't keep junk food in the house. We should take similarly extreme measures to fight our lust, Jesus says. "For it is better that you lose one of your members than that your whole body go into hell" (v. 30). A little cultural or technological amputation is far better than spiritual destruction.

### THE PORN HYDRA

When my father was an adolescent, if he had wanted to view pornography it would have required a trip to a specialty shop and face-to-face interaction with a proprietor.[25] Times have changed—drastically. Today's children and adolescents don't need to go looking for pornography; it finds them. These days, the average age at which a boy is exposed to pornography is somewhere between eight and eleven years old.[26] It's on his phone and his computer, in his video games, movies, and song lyrics. It's easier to find than the local weather forecast.[27] Philosopher and apologist Nancy Pearcey

---

25. The first *Playboy* magazine was published in 1953. The very term *playboy* is an assault on biblical masculinity, summoning men to aspire for perpetual *boy*hood with the life-long goal of *play*. See Pearcey, *Toxic War on Masculinity*, 201.

26. See Smith, *(Un)Intentional*, 8; Pearcey, *Toxic War on Masculinity*, 24–25; Morell and Littlejohn, "Parents Can't Fight Porn Alone," 35. Porn is a problem for men and women, boys and girls, though studies continue to show that males are more likely to consume porn regularly. See, for example, Cox et al., "How Prevalent Is Pornography?"

27. Reinke, *12 Ways Your Phone Is Changing You*, 134. Haidt, *Anxious Generation*, 187, says that by the late 1990s, perhaps as much as 40 percent of all

explains that porn is so pervasive that when a group of researchers tried to conduct a study on its effects, they were unable to find enough men in their twenties who had *not* watched porn to form a control group.[28] A minor using Snapchat can reach a pornographic site in just five clicks, without ever leaving the app.[29] A significant portion of online porn is dirt cheap, or even free. Researchers often speak of "the three As of internet pornography": *accessibility, affordability,* and *anonymity*.[30] Indubitably, the first two are true. But the third—anonymity—is one of the great lies of the internet age. Technology makes us think we can indulge in vices anonymously, safe from exposure and consequences. But as Tony Reinke says, "There's no such thing as anonymity. It is only a matter of time."[31]

Internet pornography is fundamentally different from earlier forms of pornography, not only in its availability, but also in its neurological potency and in its extremity. Neuroscientists have found that the richer the media—high-definition, hyperrealistic videos—the more powerful the effect, especially on the male brain. This helps to explain why internet pornography is more addictive than earlier forms.[32] William Struthers, professor of psychology at Wheaton College, has conducted extensive research on pornography and the brain. Struthers explains,

> Just as food is consumed and digested by the body, pornography is consumed by the senses and digested by the brain. In the digestive process, food is broken down so that it can supply the body with energy. Waste products are excreted to ensure the health of an organism. Similarly, pornography is taken into the brain via our senses, primarily through sight and touch. However, there is no process for "waste" products associated with

---

internet traffic was porn. James, *Digital Liturgies*, 132, cites the web research hub Statista, reporting that three of the top twenty most visited sites in the world offer "adult" content.

28. Pearcey, *Toxic War on Masculinity*, 24–25.
29. Morell and Littlejohn, "Parents Can't Fight Porn Alone," 36.
30. See, for example, Struthers, *Wired for Intimacy*, 32–36.
31. Reinke, *12 Ways Your Phone Is Changing You*, 138.
32. Grant, *Divine Sex*, 106.

pornography to be removed. Pornography and our response to it alter our brain in a way that is difficult to undo. Pornography is the consumption of sexual poison that becomes part of the fabric of the mind.[33]

In their cogent argument for collective action against pornography, Clare Morell and Brad Littlejohn express their concern about a dystopia of full access to porn for all ages, gate-kept only by exhausted parents. This is "a scenario we have rightly rejected in the cases of guns, drugs, alcohol, gambling, or tobacco," they say. "But it is exactly what we have embraced in the case of the internet and digital technology."[34] Presently, we put pornography in the same category as soft drinks: available to everyone, drink at your own discretion. "But porn, as research shows, is not digital sugar; it is digital fentanyl."[35]

Another cause for concern is the extremity of contemporary porn. Today's porn is more violent. More deviant. Internet pornography urges viewers toward increasingly hard-core videos. "Automatic pop-ups and linked advertisements create a fast-moving dynamic environment, which tantalizes the user in the heat of the moment to journey into unintended and increasingly extreme areas."[36] Clinicians make a distinction between the decisions we make in "cold" and "hot" status. Because internet pornography provides us with almost limitless choices during "hot" status, it lures us to places we would reject without hesitation in a "cold" state. "Scenes that would initially offend or horrify [us] soon become acceptable and even desirable."[37]

Surprisingly, research suggests that the majority of people struggling with the compulsive consumption of online pornography are *married* men.[38] And like a cancer within the body, this

33. Struthers, *Wired for Intimacy*, 20.
34. Morell and Littlejohn, "Parents Can't Fight Porn Alone," 35.
35. Morell and Littlejohn, "Parents Can't Fight Porn Alone," 38.
36. Grant, *Divine Sex*, 106.
37. Grant, *Divine Sex*, 107. Similarly, Morell and Littlejohn, "Parents Can't Fight Porn Alone," 36.
38. Grant, *Divine Sex*, 109.

pornographic poison is destroying marriages. Another of the great deceptions of pornography is its promise to satisfy sexual desire while ultimately killing it. The chronic user becomes so dependent on extreme imagery to arouse him that he is no longer attracted enough to his wife to be intimate with her. *Real life* and a *real wife* can't compete with fantasy.[39]

On June 3, 1956, C. S. Lewis wrote a letter to one of his American readers named Keith Masson, addressing the topics of lust and masturbation. Lewis replies to Masson,

> For me the real evil of masturbation would be that it takes an appetite which, in lawful use, leads the individual out of himself to complete (and correct) his own personality in that of another (and finally in children and even grandchildren) and turns it back: sends the man back into the prison of himself, there to keep a harem of imaginary brides. And this harem, once admitted, works against his *ever* getting out and really uniting with a real woman. For the harem is always accessible, always subservient, calls for no sacrifices or adjustments, and can be endowed with erotic and psychological attractions which no real woman can rival. Among those shadowy brides he is always adored, always the perfect lover: no demand is made on his unselfishness, no mortification ever imposed on his vanity. In the end, they become merely the medium through which he increasingly adores himself.[40]

## "SHALL I KILL IT?"

How does one fight lust? How does one battle the porn hydra? First, by rejecting the myriad lies of our sex-crazed culture. "Do not be conformed to this world," Paul says (Rom 12:2). Reject the lie that having *more* sex with *more* partners makes you *more* of a man. Jesus is the manliest man who ever walked the earth, and Jesus is a virgin. Let that sink in, fellas. Reject the lie that women

---

39. See Haidt, *Anxious Generation*, 188. Wolf, "Porn Myth," quips, "Today, real naked women are just bad porn."

40. Lewis, *Narnia, Cambridge, and Joy*, 758.

should behave like porn stars. The women in porn are never tired, never pregnant, always up for anything. Real women aren't like this. When Paul tells married believers not to deprive one another sexually (1 Cor 7:1–5), he doesn't mean that wives should be as available as the pornography on their husbands' iPhones.[41]

Additionally, Christians should think practically about how to avoid pornography and how to stop if they've developed a habit of consumption: tear out the eye; cut off the hand (Matt 5:29–30). Turn off the film; extinguish the glow of the phone. I'm a proponent of accountability apps like Covenant Eyes, which we've installed on all devices in our home. It's good for my wife and me to get a report of each other's internet wanderings. It's good for our adolescent sons to know that their digital footprints are being tracked. But the porn hydra cannot be defeated simply by slicing off head after head. Hercules defeated the multi-headed monster by *searing* the severed necks to prevent regeneration.[42] Block one path to porn and two more will appear. Vital for victory is the transformation of the heart: *mortification* of sin and *vivification* of sexual desire.

In Lewis's dream-story *The Great Divorce*, one Ghost carries on his shoulder a little red lizard, always twitching its tail like a whip and whispering things in the Ghost's ear. A flaming figure appears and inquires, "Would you like me to make him quiet?" "Of course I would," says the Ghost. "Then I will kill him," the Angel replies. But as the Angel begins to deal with the lizard, the process brings pain to the Ghost, causing him to retreat. "Don't you *want* him killed?" the Angel asks. "You didn't say anything about *killing* him at first. I hardly meant to bother you with anything so drastic as that," the Ghost says. But the Angel insists that this is the only way, and he brings his burning hands close to the lizard. "Shall I kill it?" Again, the Ghost hesitates: "For the moment I was only thinking about silencing it." And again the Angel inquires, "May I kill it?" "Please—really—don't bother. Look! It's gone to sleep of its own accord. I'm sure it'll be all right now. Thanks ever so much."

---

41. Wagner, *Non-Toxic Masculinity*, 169.
42. Hamilton, *Mythology*, 178–79.

## Deathly (De)Vices

This back and forth continues for a while. Finally, the Ghost gives his permission. The very moment he surrenders, he gives a scream of agony. The Angel closes his fiery grip on the lizard, breaks its back, and flings it to the ground. The Ghost, at long last free of the reptile, transforms into a solid and immense man. The lizard, too, takes a new form. It morphs into a mighty stallion, silvery white with a main and tail of gold, rippled with muscle. The new-made man leaps upon the stallion's back, and horse and master disappear into the rose-brightness of the everlasting morning.[43]

When the red lizard of lust is slain, we are liberated; and desire is reborn as the God-given and thus far greater libido that seeks the one-flesh, whole-life union of marriage.

---

43. Lewis, *Great Divorce*, 106–12.

# 9

# Conclusion

## "Now I See"

### THE BLINDING EFFECT OF OUR DEVICES

FOR AS LONG AS I can remember, I've wanted to walk like Jesus. Metaphorically, in the sense of conducting myself like him. But also, *actually* walking like him, at his speed. Some of us walk very slowly, and maybe that's why we're perpetually late. Others of us walk very quickly, hurried along by the tyranny of unaccomplished tasks. Throughout the Gospels, Jesus' walk is just right: never too quick; never too slow. Like Gandalf, he arrives precisely when he means to.

Once, as he was walking, Jesus saw a man blind from birth (John 9:1-7). His disciples, they too noticed the blind man and assumed that either he or his parents must have done something horrible to bring this suffering upon him. On the contrary, Jesus explains that this man's suffering is not associated with some specific sin, but with God's hitherto mysterious plan. "It was not that this man sinned, or his parents, but that the works of God might be displayed in him" (v. 3). Jesus then repeats what he said in the previous chapter, "I am the light of the world" (v. 5). He has said it; now he will show it.

In a strange and unhygienic display of divine power, Jesus heals the blind man. "He spit on the ground and made mud with the saliva. Then he anointed the man's eyes with the mud and said to him, 'Go, wash in the pool of Siloam'" (vv. 6–7). The reason for the pool is clear enough. The word *Siloam* means Sent. The name of the pool hints at the identity of the healer: Jesus is the Sent Son of God. The mud is less obvious, but equally important in the story. Jesus takes his saliva, some of himself, and mixes it with the dirt, some of the earth, and the result is healing. It's a picture, a miniature, of Jesus' mission. He enters his creation in order to heal it.

The God who in the beginning created light, separating the light from the darkness, on this day separates the blind man from the darkness he had known all his life. Think of the things this man never had seen. He had never seen a bird fly or a flower bloom. He had never seen another human being. Never seen amber eyes or a smiling face. He had never seen himself. What was it like, I wonder, washing his eyes, and suddenly seeing all of this for the first time?

The more I meditate on this story from John's Gospel, the more I notice similarities between the man blind from birth and digital natives. Life-long, untempered attachment to our devices has a blinding effect on us, depriving us of our ability to see the world, our fellow humans, and even ourselves rightly—as God intends for us to see, as he intends for us to *be*. Technology giveth, and technology taketh away. Technology *enables*, and technology *disables*.

My prayer is that this volume and others like it will help readers both young and old perceive the *de*-formative potential of our devices. *De*-formative potential doesn't mean that we should reject all technology outright; but it does mean that we should operate with caution. Throughout this work, I've sought to help my readers become more anchored in and enlivened by the scriptural story. I've encouraged certain rhythms of abiding in Jesus and suggested some principles of (dis)engagement with respect to various technologies. I've tried not to be overly prescriptive, recognizing that each person or family will need to think through these issues

## CONCLUSION

carefully.¹ I hope that at least some of us now see things at least somewhat more clearly than before, that conversations between husbands and wives and parents and children will commence, and that new practices will follow. The way forward is not blind tech-optimism, nor the extreme tech-pessimism of the Luddites, but *tech-pragmatism*.²

### NO EMAIL IN HEAVEN

In his final days on earth, Tim Keller left a message to those who sent him an email. His out-of-the-office reply read: "I am no longer answering email as I am in heaven and we do not use it here. In Him, Tim."³

I hope Tim was right, because at this very moment I've got heaps of emails to answer. But as I type these final words, the clock reads 5:00 p.m., and it's Friday—family night. So the emails can wait. It's time for the computer to slumber, for the iPhone to go to the time-out corner, for the AirPods to become silent. It's time for dinner, for prayer and conversation, for reading and reminiscing, for laughing so hard that someone spews their drink. This is the deeply human stuff.

---

1. For those who wish I had been more prescriptive, offering the reader a list of "rules," "guidelines," or "commitments," you will find help in Crouch, *Tech-Wise Family*; Song, *Restless Devices*, 191–211; Haidt, *Anxious Generation*, 221–88, and especially 289–95, where he recapitulates his four foundational reforms: (1) no smartphones before high school; (2) no social media before age sixteen; (3) phone-free schools; and (4) far more unsupervised play and childhood independence.

2. Probably, Postman, *Amusing Ourselves to Death*, is right: "Americans will not shut down any part of their technological apparatus, and to suggest that they do so is to make no suggestion at all" (158). "The solution," he says, "must be found in *how* we watch" (160, emphasis original).

3. Collins, *Road to Wisdom*, 173.

# Bibliography

Alter, Adam. *Irresistible: The Rise of Addictive Technology and the Business of Keeping Us Hooked*. New York: Penguin, 2018.

Aral, Sinan. *The Hype Machine: How Social Media Disrupts Our Elections, Our Economy, and Our Health—and How We Must Adapt*. New York: Currency, 2021.

Bail, Chris. *Breaking the Social Media Prism: How to Make Our Platforms Less Polarizing*. Princeton: Princeton University Press, 2021.

Barton, Bernadette. *The Pornification of America: How Raunch Culture Is Ruining Our Society*. New York: New York University Press, 2021.

Beaty, Katelyn. *Celebrities for Jesus: How Personas, Platforms, and Profits Are Hurting the Church*. Grand Rapids: Brazos, 2022.

Bergeson, Samantha. "'Poor Things' Sex Scene Re-Edited for U.K. Release." *IndieWire*, Jan. 25, 2024. https://www.indiewire.com/news/general-news/poor-things-sex-scene-reedited-uk-release-1234940615/.

Berry, Jeffrey M., and Sarah Sobieraj. *The Outrage Industry: Political Opinion Media and the New Incivility*. Oxford: Oxford University Press, 2014.

Berry, Wendell. "Family Work." In *Essays 1969–1990*, edited by Jack Shoemaker, 490–94. New York: Library of America, 2019.

———. "Feminism, the Body, and the Machine." In *Essays 1969–1990*, edited by Jack Shoemaker, 733–50. New York: Library of America, 2019.

———. *Hannah Coulter*. Berkeley: Counterpoint, 2004.

———. "Horse-Drawn Tools and the Doctrine of Labor Saving." In *Essays 1969–1990*, edited by Jack Shoemaker, 473–79. New York: Library of America, 2019.

———. *Jayber Crow*. Berkeley: Counterpoint, 2000.

———. "The Joy of Sales Resistance." In *Sex, Economy, Freedom and Community*, ix–xxi. Berkeley: Counterpoint, 1992.

———. "The Long-Legged House." In *Essays 1969–1990*, edited by Jack Shoemaker, 14–65. New York: Library of America, 2019.

———. "Out of Your Car, Off Your Horse." In *Sex, Economy, Freedom and Community*, 19–26. Berkeley: Counterpoint, 1992.

———. *The Peace of Wild Things and Other Poems*. London: Penguin, 2018.

———. "Think Little." In *Essays 1969–1990*, edited by Jack Shoemaker, 135–44. New York: Library of America, 2019.

———. "Why I Am Not Going to Buy a Computer." In *Essays 1969–1990*, edited by Jack Shoemaker, 725–32. New York: Library of America, 2019.

Bierce, Ambrose. *The Devil's Dictionary, Tales, and Memoirs*. Edited by S. T. Joshi. New York: Library of America, 2011.

Boorstin, Daniel J. *The Image: A Guide to Pseudo-Events in America*. New York: Vintage, 1992.

Borgmann, Albert. *Power Failure*. Grand Rapids: Baker, 2003.

———. *Technology and the Character of Contemporary Life: A Philosophical Inquiry*. Chicago: University of Chicago Press, 1987.

Braudy, Leo. *The Frenzy of Renown: Fame and Its History*. New York: Vintage, 1986.

The Brothers Grimm. *Snow White and Other Grimms' Fairy Tales*. New York: HarperCollins, 2022.

Brown, Raymond E. *The Epistles of John*. New Haven: Yale University Press, 1982.

Bruce, F. F. *The Epistles to the Colossians, to Philemon, and to the Ephesians*. Grand Rapids: Eerdmans, 1984.

Burton, Tara Isabella. *Self-Made: Creating Our Identities from Da Vinci to the Kardashians*. New York: PublicAffairs, 2023.

Carr, Nicholas. *The Shallows: What the Internet Is Doing to Our Brains*. Updated ed. New York: Norton, 2020.

Carson, D. A. *The Gospel According to John*. Grand Rapids: Eerdmans, 1991.

———. *Jesus's Sermon on the Mount and His Confrontation with the World: A Study of Matthew 5–10*. Grand Rapids: Baker, 2018.

Cave, Damien. "What We Gained (and Lost) When Our Daughter Unplugged for a School Year." *New York Times*, Mar. 22, 2024. https://www.nytimes.com/2024/03/22/world/australia/screen-free-school.html.

Chapman, Gary, and Arlene Pellicane. *Growing Up Social: Raising Relational Kids in a Screen-Driven World*. Chicago: Northfield, 2014.

Collins, Francis S. *The Road to Wisdom: On Truth, Science, Faith, and Trust*. New York: Little, Brown and Company, 2024.

Cox, Daniel, et al. "How Prevalent Is Pornography?" Institute for Family Studies, May 3, 2022. https://ifstudies.org/blog/how-prevalent-is-pornography.

Crouch, Amy, and Andy Crouch. *My Tech-Wise Life: Growing Up and Making Choices in a World of Devices*. Grand Rapids: Baker, 2020.

Crouch, Andy. "The Alchemists' Dream: Three Judgments About Technology." In *Technē: Christian Visions of Technology*, edited by Gerald Hiestand and Todd A. Wilson, 36–60. Eugene, OR: Cascade, 2022.

———. "It's Time to Reckon with Celebrity Power." The Gospel Coalition, Mar. 24, 2018. https://www.thegospelcoalition.org/article/time-reckon-celebrity-power/?amp.

———. *The Life We're Looking For: Reclaiming Relationship in a Technological World*. New York: Convergent, 2022.

# BIBLIOGRAPHY

———. *The Tech-Wise Family: Everyday Steps for Putting Technology in Its Proper Place*. Grand Rapids: Baker, 2017.
Currid-Halkett, Elizabeth. *Starstruck: The Business of Celebrity*. New York: Faber & Faber, 2010.
DeYoung, Kevin. *Crazy Busy*. Wheaton, IL: Crossway, 2013.
———. "Technology Is Neither Good, nor Bad, nor Neutral with Tony Reinke and Samuel James." *Life and Books and Everything* podcast, episode 122, aired Apr. 27, 2023.
DeYoung, Rebecca Konyndyk. *Glittering Vices: A New Look at the Seven Deadly Sins and Their Remedies*. Grand Rapids: Brazos, 2020.
———. *Vainglory: The Forgotten Vice*. Grand Rapids: Eerdmans, 2014.
Dickens, Charles. *A Christmas Carol*. Moscow, ID: Canon, 2020.
Dickerson, Matthew. "Wendell Berry, C. S. Lewis, J. R. R. Tolkien and the Dangers of a Technological Mindset." *Flourish*, Fall 2010. https://flourishonline.org/2010/12/wendell-berry-cs-lewis-jrr-tolkien-and-the-dangers-of-a-technological-mindset/.
Dixhoorn, Chad Van. *Confessing the Faith*. Carlisle, PA: Banner of Truth, 2014.
Dizikes, Peter. "Study: On Twitter, False News Travels Faster Than True Stories." *MIT News*, Mar. 8, 2018. https://news.mit.edu/2018/study-twitter-false-news-travels-faster-true-stories-0308.
Douglas, Susan J., and Andrea McDonnell. *Celebrity: A History of Fame*. New York: New York University Press, 2019.
Dyer, John. *People of the Screen: How Evangelicals Created the Digital Bible and How it Shapes Their Reading of Scripture*. New York: Oxford University Press, 2023.
Ellul, Jacques. *The Technological Society*. New York: Vintage, 1964.
Estes, Douglas, ed. *Theology and Tolkien: Practical Theology*. Lanham, MD: Lexington, 2023.
Eyal, Nir. *Hooked: How to Build Habit-Forming Products*. New York: Portfolio, 2014.
Finkel, Michael. "The Science of Sleep." *National Geographic*, Aug. 2018.
Fisher, Helen. *Anatomy of Love: A Natural History of Mating, Marriage, and Why We Stray*. New York: Norton, 2016.
Fisher, Max. *The Chaos Machine: The Inside Story of How Social Media Rewired Our Minds and Our World*. New York: Little, Brown and Company, 2022.
Fradd, Matt. *The Porn Myth: Exposing the Reality Behind the Fantasy of Pornography*. San Francisco: Ignatius, 2017.
France, R. T. *The Gospel of Matthew*. Grand Rapids: Eerdmans, 2011.
Garrett, Duane A. *A Commentary on Exodus*. Grand Rapids: Kregel Academic, 2014.
Goldberg, Emma. "The ZIP Code Shift: Why Many Americans No Longer Live Where They Work." *New York Times*, Mar. 4, 2024. https://www.nytimes.com/2024/03/04/business/zip-code-shift-home-work.html.
Grant, Jonathan. *Divine Sex: A Compelling Vision for Christian Relationships in a Hypersexualized Age*. Grand Rapids: Brazos, 2015.

# BIBLIOGRAPHY

Haidt, Jonathan. *The Anxious Generation: How the Great Rewiring of Childhood Is Causing an Epidemic of Mental Illness*. New York: Penguin, 2024.

Hamilton, Edith. *Mythology: Timeless Tales of Gods and Heroes*. New York: Black Dog & Leventhal, 1942.

Hamilton, Victor P. *The Book of Genesis*. Grand Rapids: Eerdmans, 1990.

Harber, Ian. "Social Media Is a Spiritual Distortion Zone." The Gospel Coalition, Aug. 11, 2023. https://www.thegospelcoalition.org/article/social-media-spiritual-distortion/.

Hari, Johann. *Stolen Focus: Why You Can't Pay Attention—And How to Think Deeply Again*. New York: Crown, 2022.

Harlem World. "The Legendary Collyer Brothers Harlem NY 1881–1947." Nov. 6, 2020. https://www.harlemworldmagazine.com/the-legendary-collyer-brothers-harlem-ny-1881-1947-rare-video/.

Hauerwas, Stanley. *Matthew*. Grand Rapids: Brazos, 2006.

Hawgood, Alex. "What Is 'Bigorexia'?" *New York Times*, Mar. 5, 2022. https://www.nytimes.com/2022/03/05/style/teen-bodybuilding-bigorexia-tiktok.html.

Herring, Scott. *The Hoarders: Material Deviance in Modern American Culture*. Chicago: University of Chicago Press, 2014.

Hiestand, Gerald, and Todd Wilson, eds. *Beauty, Order, and Mystery: A Christian Vision of Human Sexuality*. Downers Grove, IL: IVP Academic, 2017.

———, eds. *Technē: Christian Visions of Technology*. Eugene, OR: Cascade, 2022.

Horwitz, Jeff, and Deepa Seetharaman. "Facebook Executives Shut Down Efforts to Make the Site Less Divisive." *Wall Street Journal*, May 26, 2020. https://www.wsj.com/articles/facebook-knows-it-encourages-division-top-executives-nixed-solutions-11590507499?st=5clb6mhjf9iujo1&reflink=share_mobilewebshare.

Hughes, R. Kent, and Barbara Hughes. *Liberating Ministry from the Success Syndrome*. Wheaton, IL: Crossway, 2008.

Hund, Emily. *The Influencer Industry: The Quest for Authenticity on Social Media*. Princeton: Princeton University Press, 2023.

IMDb. "Poor Things (2023)." https://www.imdb.com/title/tt14230458/?ref_=nv_sr_srsg_0_tt_7_nm_1_in_0_q_poor%25othing.

Irving, Washington. *The Legend of Sleepy Hollow and Other Stories*. New York: Penguin, 1988.

Isaacson, Walter. *Steve Jobs*. New York: Simon & Schuster, 2011.

James, Samuel. *Digital Liturgies: Rediscovering Christian Wisdom in an Online Age*. Wheaton, IL: Crossway, 2023.

Jobes, Karen H. *1, 2, and 3 John*. Grand Rapids: Zondervan, 2014.

Johnson, Luke Timothy. *The First and Second Letters to Timothy*. Anchor Bible 35A. New Haven: Yale University Press, 2008.

———. *The Letter of James*. New Haven: Yale University Press, 1995.

# Bibliography

Johnson, Rian, dir. *Glass Onion: A Knives Out Mystery*. Los Angeles: T-Street Productions; Netflix, 2022.

———. *Star Wars: Episode VIII—The Last Jedi*. Lucasfilm Ltd. Burbank, CA: Walt Disney Studios, 2017.

Jones, Beth Felker. *Faithful: A Theology of Sex*. Grand Rapids: Zondervan, 2015.

Kapic, Kelly. *You're Only Human: How Your Limits Reflect God's Design and Why That's Good News*. Grand Rapids: Brazos, 2022.

Kardaras, Nicholas. *Glow Kids: How Screen Addiction Is Hijacking Our Kids—And How to Break the Trance*. Repr. ed. New York: St. Martin's Griffin, 2017.

Keller, Timothy. *Forgive: Why Should I and How Can I?* New York: Penguin, 2022.

———. *The Meaning of Marriage: Facing the Complexities of Commitment with the Wisdom of God*. New York: Penguin, 2013.

Kelly, Kevin. *What Technology Wants*. New York: Penguin, 2011.

Kidner, Derek. *Genesis*. Downers Grove, IL: IVP Academic, 1967.

———. *Proverbs*. Downers Grove, IL: IVP Academic, 2018.

Kim, Jay Y. *Analog Christian: Cultivating Contentment, Resilience, and Wisdom in the Digital Age*. Downers Grove, IL: InterVarsity, 2022.

King, Don W., ed. *The Collected Poems of C. S. Lewis: A Critical Edition*. Kent, OH: Kent State University Press, 2015.

Kinnaman, David, et al. *Faith for Exiles: 5 Ways for a New Generation to Follow Jesus in Digital Babylon*. Grand Rapids: Baker, 2019.

Klein, Ezra. "How Technology Is Designed to Bring Out the Worst in Us." *Vox*, Feb. 19, 2018. https://www.vox.com/technology/2018/2/19/17020310/tristan-harris-facebook-twitter-humane-tech-time.

Köstenberger, Andreas J. *John*. Grand Rapids: Baker Academic, 2004.

Kranzberg, Melvin. "Technology and History: 'Kranzberg's Laws.'" *Technology and Culture* 27 (1986) 544–650.

Kreider, Tim. "Isn't It Outrageous?" *New York Times*, July 14, 2009. https://archive.nytimes.com/opinionator.blogs.nytimes.com/2009/07/14/isnt-it-outrageous/?searchResultPosition=1.

Lamott, Anne. *Traveling Mercies: Some Thoughts on Faith*. New York: Anchor, 1999.

Lanier, Jaron. *Ten Arguments for Deleting Your Social Media Accounts Right Now*. New York: Picador, 2019.

Lewis, C. S. "Christian Apologetics." In *C. S. Lewis Essay Collection: Faith, Christianity and the Church*, edited by Lesley Walmsley, 147–59. Hammersmith: HarperCollins, 2002.

———. *The Four Loves*. New York: Harcourt, 1960.

———. *The Great Divorce*. New York: HarperOne, 1946.

———. *Mere Christianity*. New York: HarperCollins, 1952.

———. *Narnia, Cambridge, and Joy, 1950–1963*. Vol. 3 of *The Collected Letters of C. S. Lewis*. Edited by Walter Hooper. New York: HarperCollins, 2007.

———. *Perelandra*. New York: Scribner, 1944.

# BIBLIOGRAPHY

Lieber, Chavie. "How and Why Do Influencers Make So Much Money?" *Vox*, Nov. 28, 2018. https://www.vox.com/the-goods/2018/11/28/18116875/influencer-marketing-social-media-engagement-instagram-youtube.

Lucky, Kate. "AI Will Shape Your Soul." *Christianity Today*, 2023. https://www.christianitytoday.com/ct/2023/october/artificial-intelligence-robots-soul-formation.html.

Lustig, Robert H. *Fat Chance: Beating the Odds Against Sugar, Processed Food, Obesity, and Disease*. New York: Hudson Street, 2012.

Lusvardi, Anthony R. "Screens and Sacraments." *First Things*, Nov. 2024.

Marantz, Andrew. *Antisocial: Online Extremists, Techno-Utopians, and the Hijacking of the American Conversation*. New York: Viking, 2019.

Marcus, Sharon. *The Drama of Celebrity*. Princeton: Princeton University Press, 2019.

Marshall, I. Howard. *The Epistles of John*. Grand Rapids: Eerdmans, 1978.

Martin, Chris. *The Wolf in Their Pockets: 13 Ways the Social Internet Threatens the People You Lead*. Chicago: Moody, 2023.

Marwick, Alice E. *Status Update: Celebrity, Publicity, and Branding in the Social Media Age*. New Haven: Yale University Press, 2015.

McCracken, Brett. "How to Avoid Anger Overload in the Digital Age." The Gospel Coalition, July 15, 2019. https://www.thegospelcoalition.org/article/anger-overload-digital-age/?amp.

———. *The Wisdom Pyramid: Feeding Your Soul in a Post-Truth World*. Wheaton, IL: Crossway, 2021.

McCracken, Sandra. "Dying to Our Selfies." *Christianity Today*, Nov. 2023.

McKelvey, Douglas Kaine. *Every Moment Holy*. Vol. 1. Nashville: Rabbit Room, 2017.

McNamee, Roger. *Zucked: Waking Up to the Facebook Catastrophe*. New York: Penguin, 2019.

Mills, Elle. "YouTube Gave Me Everything. Then I Grew Up." *New York Times*, Feb. 5, 2023. https://www.nytimes.com/2023/02/05/opinion/elle-mills-youtube-quit.html.

Moo, Douglas J. *The Letter of James*. Grand Rapids: Eerdmans, 2000.

Morell, Clare, and Brad Littlejohn. "Parents Can't Fight Porn Alone." *First Things*, Feb. 2025.

Morris, Leon. *The Gospel According to Matthew*. Grand Rapids: Eerdmans, 1992.

Newport, Cal. *Digital Minimalism: Choosing a Focused Life in a Noisy World*. New York: Portfolio, 2019.

Nichols, Tom. *The Death of Expertise: The Campaign Against Established Knowledge and Why It Matters*. Oxford: Oxford University Press, 2018.

Nodder, Chris. *Evil by Design: Interaction Design to Lead Us into Temptation*. Indianapolis: Wiley, 2013.

Nolan, Christopher, dir. *Inception*. Burbank, CA: Warner Brothers Pictures, 2010.

# Bibliography

Norman, Alex. "Celebrity Push, Celebrity Pull: Understanding the Role of the Notable Person in Pilgrimage." *Journal for the Academic Study of Religion* 24 (2011) 317–41.

Ordway, Holly. *Tolkien's Faith: A Spiritual Biography*. Park Ridge, IL: Word on Fire Academic, 2023.

———. *Tolkien's Modern Reading: Middle-Earth Beyond the Middle Ages*. Park Ridge, IL: Word on Fire Academic, 2021.

Parker, Andrew, and Nick J. Watson. "Sport, Celebrity and Religion: Christianity, Morality and the Tebow Phenomenon." *Studies in World Christianity* 21 (2015) 223–38.

Pearcey, Nancy R. *Love Thy Body: Answering Hard Questions About Life and Sexuality*. Grand Rapids: Baker, 2018.

———. *The Toxic War on Masculinity: How Christianity Reconciles the Sexes*. Grand Rapids: Baker, 2023.

Postman, Neil. *Amusing Ourselves to Death: Public Discourse in the Age of Show Business*. New York: Penguin, 2005.

Powlison, David. *Good and Angry: Redeeming Anger, Irritation, Complaining, and Bitterness*. Greensboro, NC: New Growth, 2016.

Price, Catherine. *How to Break Up with Your Phone*. New York: Ten Speed, 2018.

Prior, Karen Swallow. "The Christian Woman's Path to Power." *Christianity Today*, Nov. 2019.

Read, Max. "How MrBeast Became the Willy Wonka of YouTube." *New York Times*, June 12, 2023. https://www.nytimes.com/2023/06/12/magazine/mrbeast-youtube.html.

Reinke, Tony. *12 Ways Your Phone Is Changing You*. Wheaton, IL: Crossway, 2017.

———. *God, Technology, and the Christian Life*. Wheaton, IL: Crossway, 2022.

Rose-Stockwell, Tobias. *Outrage Machine: How Tech Amplifies Discontent, Disrupts Democracy—and What We Can Do About It*. New York: Legacy Lit, 2023.

Schindler, D. C. "Social Media Is Hate Speech: A Platonic Reflection on Contemporary Misology." *Humanum*, Sept. 17, 2020. https://humanumreview.com/articles/social-media-is-hate-speech.

Smith, Christian, and Hilary Davidson. *The Paradox of Generosity: Giving We Receive, Grasping We Lose*. Oxford: Oxford University Press, 2014.

Smith, Doug. *(Un)Intentional: How Screens Secretly Shape Your Desires and How You Can Break Free*. Grand Rapids: Credo House, 2021.

Smith, Justin E. H. *The Internet Is Not What You Think It Is: A History, a Philosophy, a Warning*. Princeton: Princeton University Press, 2022.

Smith, Ted A. "Political Theology Through a History of Preaching: A Study in the Authority of Celebrity." *Homiletic* 42 (2017) 18–34.

Snodgrass, Klyne R. *Stories with Intent: A Comprehensive Guide to the Parables of Jesus*. Grand Rapids: Eerdmans, 2008.

# Bibliography

Song, Felicia Wu. "Digital Life and Social Media as Secular Liturgy." In *Technē: Christian Visions of Technology*, edited by Gerald Hiestand and Todd A. Wilson, 202–20. Eugene, OR: Cascade, 2022.

———. *Restless Devices: Recovering Personhood, Presence, and Place in the Digital Age*. Downers Grove, IL: IVP Academic, 2021.

Sorkin, Aaron, dir. *Being the Ricardos*. Culver City, CA: Amazon Studios, 2021.

Sosler, Alex. "The Culture Wars and The Lord of the Rings: Models of Christian Engagement." In *Theology and Tolkien: Practical Theology*, edited by Douglas Estes, 135–49. Lanham, MD: Lexington, 2023.

Stahelski, Chad, dir. *John Wick: Chapter 4*. Santa Monica, CA: Lionsgate Films, 2023.

Stephens, Mark B., and Georgiane Deal. "The God Who Gives Generously: Honour, Praise and the Agony of Celebrity." *Scottish Journal of Theology* 71 (2018) 52–66.

Stokel-Walker, Chris. *YouTubers: How YouTube Shook Up TV and Created a New Generation of Stars*. Surrey: Canbury, 2019.

Storr, Will. *Selfie: How We Became So Self-Obsessed and What It's Doing to Us*. New York: Abrams, 2019.

Stott, John. *The Message of the Sermon on the Mount*. Rev. ed. Downers Grove, IL: IVP Academic, 2020.

Struthers, William M. *Wired for Intimacy: How Pornography Hijacks the Male Brain*. Downers Grove, IL: IVP, 2009.

Thielman, Frank. *Ephesians*. Grand Rapids: Baker Academic, 2010.

———. *Theology of the New Testament: A Canonical and Synthetic Approach*. Grand Rapids: Zondervan, 2005.

Thomas, Zoe. "How Instagram's Algorithm Connects and Promotes Pedophile Network." *WSJ Tech News Briefing* podcast, June 8, 2023. https://www.wsj.com/podcasts/tech-news-briefing/how-instagrams-algorithm-connects-and-promotes-pedophile-network/a683c0b4-2e6f-4661-9973-10bd455db895.

Thompson, Derek. *Hit Makers: How to Succeed in an Age of Distraction*. New York: Penguin, 2018.

Tolkien, J. R. R. *The Fellowship of the Ring*. 2nd ed. Boston: William Morrow, 1965.

———. *The Hobbit*. Collector's ed. London: HarperCollins, 2012.

———. *Mr. Bliss*. London: HarperCollins, 2011.

Tolstoy, Leo. *The Death of Ivan Ilyich and Other Stories*. London: Penguin, 2008.

Toscano, Michael. "The Myth of Technological Neutrality." *First Things*, Oct. 2024.

Towner, Philip H. *The Letters to Timothy and Titus*. New International Commentary on the New Testament. Grand Rapids: Eerdmans, 2006.

Turkle, Sherry. *Alone Together*. New York: Basic, 2011.

———. *Reclaiming Conversation: The Power of Talk in a Digital Age*. New York: Penguin, 2015.

# Bibliography

Twenge, Jean M. *Generations: The Real Differences Between Gen Z, Millennials, Gen X, Boomers, and Silents—and What They Mean for America's Future.* New York: Atria, 2023.

———. *iGen: Why Today's Super-Connected Kids Are Growing Up Less Rebellious, More Tolerant, Less Happy—and Completely Unprepared for Adulthood—and What That Means for the Rest of Us.* New York: Atria, 2017.

Vaidhyanathan, Siva. *Antisocial Media: How Facebook Disconnects Us and Undermines Democracy.* New York: Oxford University Press, 2018.

Valentino-DeVries, Jennifer, and Michael H. Keller. "A Marketplace of Girl Influencers Managed by Moms and Stalked by Men." *New York Times*, Feb. 23, 2024. https://www.nytimes.com/2024/02/22/us/instagram-child-influencers.html.

Verbinski, Gore, dir. *Pirates of the Caribbean: The Curse of the Black Pearl.* Burbank, CA: Walt Disney Pictures, 2003.

Villodas, Rich. "The Celebrity Pastor Problem Is Every Church's Struggle." *Christianity Today*, Dec. 8, 2020. https://www.christianitytoday.com/pastors/2020/december-web-exclusives/celebrity-pastor-entitlement-church-culture-humility.html.

Volf, Miroslav. *Exclusion and Embrace: A Theological Exploration of Identity, Otherness, and Reconciliation.* Nashville: Abingdon, 2019.

Wagner, Zachary. *Non-Toxic Masculinity: Recovering Healthy Male Sexuality.* Downers Grove, IL: InterVarsity, 2023.

Walker, Matthew. *Why We Sleep: Unlocking the Power of Sleep and Dreams.* New York: Scribner, 2017.

Waltke, Bruce K. *Genesis: A Commentary.* Grand Rapids: Zondervan Academic, 2001.

Ward, Pete. *Celebrity Worship.* London: Routledge, 2020.

Watkin, Christopher. *Biblical Critical Theory: How the Bible's Unfolding Story Makes Sense of Modern Life and Culture.* Grand Rapids: Zondervan Academic, 2022.

Weinstein, Deena, and Michael Weinstein. "Celebrity Worship as Weak Religion." *Word and World* 23 (2003) 294–302.

Willard, Dallas. *Renovation of the Heart: Putting On the Character of Christ.* Colorado Springs: NavPress, 2012.

Willimon, William H. *Sinning Like a Christian: A New Look at the 7 Deadly Sins.* Nashville: Abingdon, 2005.

Wolf, Naomi. "The Porn Myth." *New York Magazine*, Oct. 9, 2003. https://nymag.com/nymetro/news/trends/n_9437/.

Wright, Christopher J. H. *Deuteronomy.* Grand Rapids: Baker, 1996.

Yarbrough, Robert W. *1–3 John.* Grand Rapids: Baker Academic, 2008.

www.ingramcontent.com/pod-product-compliance
Lightning Source LLC
Chambersburg PA
CBHW020854160426
43192CB00007B/921